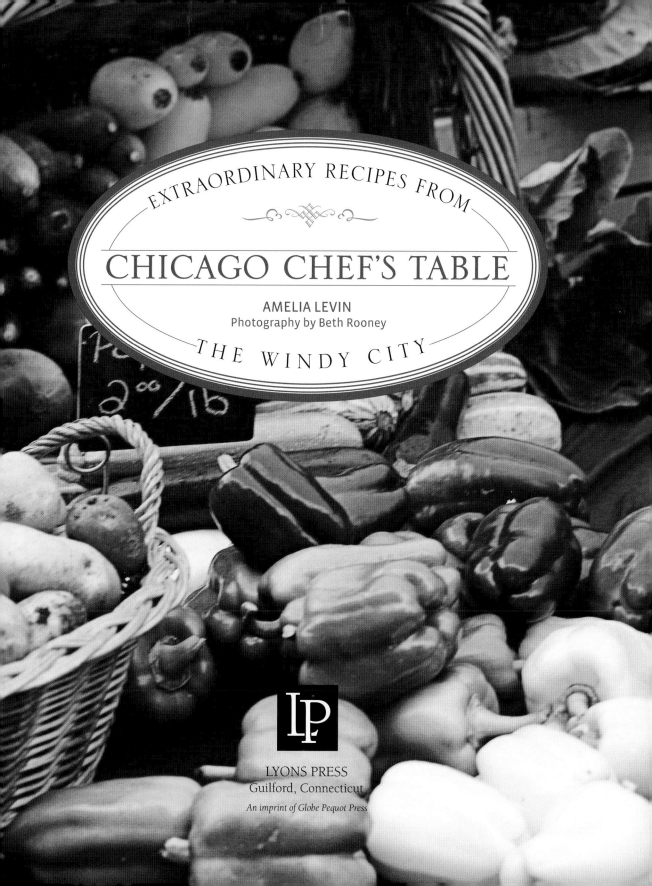

EXTRAORDINARY RECIPES FROM

CHICAGO CHEF'S TABLE

AMELIA LEVIN
Photography by Beth Rooney

THE WINDY CITY

LYONS PRESS
Guilford, Connecticut
An imprint of Globe Pequot Press

All interior photos by Beth Rooney, except page 89 courtesy of Gibsons Bar & Steakhouse; page 105, courtesy of Rockit Ranch Productions; and page 192 courtesy of Samuel Lee, Samuel Lee Photography

Text design: Sheryl P. Kober
Project editor: Julie Marsh
Layout: Nancy Freeborn

Library of Congress Cataloging-in-Publication Data is available on file.

ISBN 978-0-7627-7140-0

Printed in the United States of America

10 9 8 7 6 5 4 3 2

Restaurnats and chefs often come and go, and menus are ever-changing. We recommend you call ahead to obtain current information before visiting any of the establishments in this book.

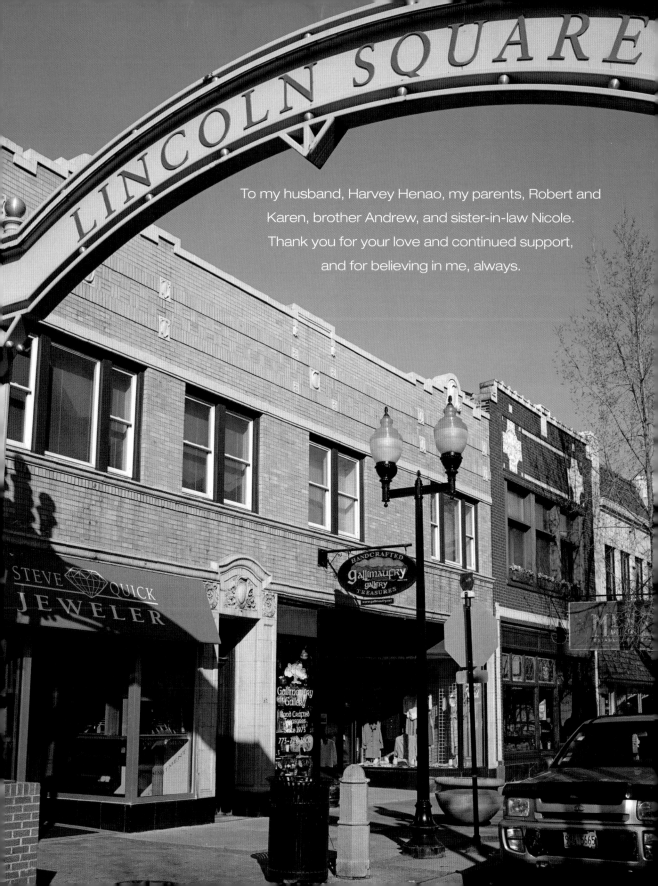

To my husband, Harvey Henao, my parents, Robert and Karen, brother Andrew, and sister-in-law Nicole. Thank you for your love and continued support, and for believing in me, always.

CONTENTS

Beef, Lamb, & More 87

Acknowledgments

"I love Chicago." In all my travels around the country and the world, I have yet to hear one person say something bad about this city. In fact, more often than not, they've used those three simple words to describe it, as if the classic I-heart-NY T-shirt had been made for us.

Chicago has a reputation for being a true Midwestern city—friendly folks, harsh winters, humid summers, and, of course, good hearty food. In the last decade, though, our "Second City" has blossomed beyond the attractions of the Mag Mile, endless skyscrapers, and pretty coastline of salt-free water. Many now look at Chicago as a culinary mecca, rich in world-class restaurants and award-winning chefs who care just as strongly as they cook.

I deeply thank the talented chefs and restaurateurs for graciously and generously contributing tested recipes for this book, and for graciously and generously feeding this city and its visitors. I also thank them for shaping Midwestern fare into what it is now—seasonally and farmers'-market driven, creative, soulful, even whimsical—and for serving as culinary leaders in this country's quest to define and refine modern American cuisine.

I also thank my editors Katie Benoit and Julie Marsh at Globe Pequot Press for their kindness, diligence, and guidance, and photographer Beth Rooney, who worked hard to capture the beauty and deliciousness of this city. And special thanks to Jenni Ferrari-Adler, my agent at Brickhouse Literary Agents, for believing in my ideas and bringing me to this talented team.

A very, very special thanks to my mom, Karen Levin, a thirty-year recipe developer who came to my side to help edit many of the book's recipes. As a member of the prestigious Les Dames d'Escoffier organization, my mother, like many women chefs featured in this book, works every day to set an example for young women aspiring to lead successful careers in the food world.

Finally, I thank my number one taste tester and fellow food lover, Harvey, my husband, who supports me day in and day out, and who makes me a better woman.

Introduction

For decades, Chicago's been looked at as second-best, the proverbial middle child, the town with the big lake and bad weather nestled quietly in the center of the Midwest, surrounded by cornfield and open land. We like cheesy, thick-crusted pizzas, accentuate our "a"s and have a tendency to be a little too loud—sometimes.

But these days, Chicago's not so second anymore. In fact, it's been deemed a culinary mecca. And there's no denying that the chefs and the food they cook have turned some eyes and raised some eyebrows.

For a city once known simply for its giant steaks and strong, blue cheese olive-spiked martinis, we've come a long way—food scene speaking, that is. While Chicagoans continue to enjoy those staple foods as much as sweet corn and heirloom tomatoes in the summer or slow-roasted beef and carrot stews in the winter, chefs here continue to push the envelope when it comes to not only experimenting with new flavors, foods, and farms, but also leading a new style of cuisine.

When I was younger, I went to a fundraising brunch put on by some of the big name chefs in the city. Then, a man named Jean who wore a white coat stamped with "Everest" had a hearty laugh and pronounced his name with a soft "j" and long "o," true to his French roots. I remember a younger chef named Charlie who smiled widely and made a joke or two as he served a buttery crepe filled with creamy goat cheese, wrapped up with chive stems like a little purse. Chef Rick peppered our taste buds with a spicy salsa over shredded duck. And little did I know a chef named Pierre Pollin from Le Titi de Paris would teach me the art of sauce making twenty years later in the belly of Kendall College's kitchens.

That was the year 1988. It was a time when the old guard was merging with the new, when the French-born chefs who laid the fine-dining foundation in Chicago were training and fusing with the up-and-coming generation. Gordon Sinclair's "new world" restaurant was becoming more popular day-by-day. And Gordon's protégé Charlie Trotter had just opened his own version of a contemporary American restaurant only a year prior. Already he was making headlines, along with Rick Bayless and his then year-old, fine-dining Mexican cuisine restaurant, Topolobampo.

It would be ten years until even more fun happened. In 1997 restaurant visionary Donnie Madia plucked Chef Paul Kahan for his Blackbird restaurant, later opening Avec next door on Randolph and arguably starting what's now deemed Restaurant Row. In 1999 Gale Gand and Rick Tramanto, who came from the legendary Trio, which would ultimately see the likes of Shawn McClain and Grant Achatz, opened fine-dining American restaurant Tru. Once the Millennium hit, Carrie Nahabedian, who also trained at Gordon alongside Charlie Trotter, opened Naha in the legendary restaurant's River North digs once it closed, not far from friend Bayless. That same year, Bruce Sherman opened North Pond on the grassy banks of Lincoln Park's northernmost pond. And so it went, year after year, chef after chef.

On the surface, what these chefs had in common was a drive and vision for inventive, creative, and experimental American cuisine that would lay the groundwork for years to come. But perhaps even more important, they shared and still share a love of Midwestern ingredients, farms, and people just like Trotter had proven with his namesake restaurant. And this was well before the "local" thing was cool. It was also certainly before the terms "green," "sustainable," and "farm-to-fork" existed.

Today, one or two generations later, those institutional restaurants have served as incubators for new waves of chefs cropping up, many of whom have not only raked in awards and reached celebrity stardom across the nation, but who also share in that love of Midwestern foods and farms.

Delicately roasted cauliflower at Stephanie Izard's Girl and the Goat. Sautéed spring ramps just emerged from the earth at Paul Virant's Vie and Perennial Virant. Indiana chicken that's slow-roasted and pulled for a tortilla soup at Province. It's about comfort, for sure, but dressed up with technique. It's about spring vegetables in the spring, summertime ones during the harvest, and wintery ones for the cold. It's about thought-out proteins, from animals raised nearby with care. It's about blending food and drink, from a cool cocktail to an approachable wine, in the spirit of some good-natured hospitality and fun. That is the essence of modern Midwestern market cuisine.

And then there's Grant. A champion of local farmers and produce, for sure, Grant Achatz has nonetheless stepped outside the confines of tradition to forge his own path into another realm of cooking and dining. In doing so, he has not only helped elevate the chefs around him (he's mentored many), he's also elevated the city's culinary scene as we now know it. Decades ago someone may have questioned his interpretation of peanut butter and jelly in the form of a liquid nitrogen-frozen grape wrapped in a thin sheet of buttery brioche bursting with juice at first bite. Now, Achatz's craftsmanship and innovation are known around the world as strokes of genius.

When Achatz won the James Beard Foundation's top honor in 2008, it seemed to spark an even more intense flutter of activity in the food scene here. With that, and a nationwide recession, came openings and closings, re-concepts, makeovers, and multiple chefs on the move, week to week, even day to day it seemed.

Now, naturally, in a fast-paced, changing food city such as Chicago, chefs will have already moved around by the time this book comes out—a testament to the dynamic nature of a burgeoning food mecca. The curious thing about Chicago chefs though, while some move around more frequently than others, most of them stay in the city.

Maybe that's because the chefs who choose to build a career here have it good. Really good. Not only is it more affordable to open up shop here compared to other big cities, there is a supportive and, frankly uncanny, camaraderie that's yet another clear definition you're in Chicago and not anywhere else. Patrick Sheerin summed up the phenomenon well: "I've been with the Signature Room for almost nine years and have been fortunate to meet so many other chefs who have grown into their positions and created this strong chef community," he said. "What's unique about this community is that, while we're still competitive, everyone is really friendly and willing to help one another."

Despite movement from restaurant to restaurant, chefs here still manage to leave their mark on their alma maters, shaping both the menu and reputation for years to come. Combined, their work has just as much significance as individuals. They don't just cook their own form of "contemporary Chicago" cuisine, together they define it.

A handful of miles outside of the city, the sun is rising and farmers are already hard at work. Some few hours later, a butcher is prepping for the busy day ahead. Legendary restaurateur Rich Melman and sons R. J. and Jerrod may be thinking about the next great concept. That said, Kevin Boehm and Rob Katz may be too. By dusk, the white coats are on, the diners are out, the city's hopping, and a server is in the weeds.

Suddenly, it becomes clear. Food is Chicago. Chicago is food. The story of the Chicago chef's table has its roots, for sure. But in many ways, it's only just beginning.

STARTERS

A longtime tradition of haute French cuisine, the *amuse-bouche*, literally "mouth amuser," signals the start of a culinary experience, allowing the chef to make a good first impression before the bread basket hits the table. Often enjoyed with a cocktail or champagne, the complimentary single-bite serving has inspired artful presentations across Chicago tables—from a crunchy crouton resting in a dollop of garlic aioli with a pork belly topper, to a spoonful of ceviche-style scallops spiked with Thai chiles, to an espresso cup filled with just a few sips of a rich herbal bisque.

From there, we move on to first courses. While the "small plates" term itself has gone in and out of fashion, the concept continues in popularity. Often masked as a long list of appetizers, these tapas-like plates, typically shared by couples or groups, may also replace full-size entrees during an evening meal. In fact, some restaurants offer half-size portions of their main dishes as guests look to not only eat lighter but also create their own "tasting menus" and broaden their palate experiences.

VIE

4471 LAWN AVENUE, WESTERN SPRINGS
(708) 246-2082
WWW.VIERESTAURANT.COM
CHEF-OWNER: PAUL VIRANT

Vie means "life" in French, and what a good one it has been for chef-owner Paul Virant. After training at Paul Kahan's legendary Blackbird, Virant moved with his wife to Western Springs at the same time Western Springs was looking for someone like him. A dry town even before the Prohibition era, the charming, quaint Western Springs, just 25 minutes from downtown Chicago, sought to bring in more family-focused restaurants and allow their alcohol sales to boost the local economy.

A family-focused man himself, known for taking his two boys on mushroom foraging outings and farm visits, Virant has extended that focus at Vie, which attracts many local families as well as young married couples, empty nesters, and a handful of city dwellers looking for the sophistication they get at home, but in a quieter setting.

In the main dining room, white-painted walls, white tablecloths, and quilted black leather banquettes exude the elegance of a fine-dining French restaurant paired with simple, straight-from-the-farm meals prepared using the classic cooking techniques one would expect from the Michelin-starred chef. Aside from his label as award-winning chef and one of the leaders of the farm-to-table movement long before that phrase existed, Virant also acts as in-house butcher—working with local farmers who provide whole animals he'll use for everything from pâtés and other delicacy dishes to steaks and chops. Virant also serves as an educator, famous for his cooking and canning classes that, lately, he's taken to his regulars' homes. "If you're eating seasonally in the Midwest, you need to do some kind of preservation so you can eat locally all year round." In this recipe he pickles green beans for a seasonal salad.

Harvest Salad with Quick-Pickled Summer Beans
(Serves 4)

For the quick-pickled summer beans:

1 pound summer beans (green beans and/or
    yellow wax beans), trimmed and washed
1 cup water
2 cups champagne vinegar
2 teaspoons sugar
1 teaspoon kosher salt
1 teaspoon crushed red pepper flakes
3 sprigs fresh dill
1 teaspoon dill seed
1 teaspoon black peppercorns
3 cloves garlic, peeled

For the salad:

2 tablespoons grapeseed oil
1 cup trimmed, cored, and quartered
    brussels sprouts
2 cups pickled beans
1 medium hakuri turnip (or salad turnip),
    trimmed and thinly sliced
1 medium Honey Crisp apple, sliced
1 small red onion, thinly sliced
1 cup flat-leaf parsley leaves
¼ cup extra-virgin olive oil
Kosher salt and pepper, to taste
Rustic croutons and freshly grated pecorino
    Romano cheese (optional garnish)

Blanch the beans in a large pot of boiling salted water for 1 minute; drain. Place beans in a container large enough to hold brine. Combine remaining 9 ingredients in a saucepan and bring to a boil. Pour brine over beans. The liquid should cover the beans (to help cover, place a large resealable plastic bag filled with water on top). Cool completely and refrigerate. Beans are ready immediately, but could be prepared up to a week ahead.

Strain the beans, reserving ¼ cup of the pickled bean liquid. Bring this liquid to a boil in a small saucepan and reduce by half. Set aside.

Heat the grapeseed oil over medium-high heat in a large sauté pan. Add brussels sprouts and cook until caramelized and tender, about 5 minutes. Transfer to a medium bowl and cool.

Add the beans, turnip, apple, onion, and parsley to the brussels sprouts. Whisk together olive oil, reduced bean liquid, salt, and pepper. Add dressing to bowl, toss to coat. Divide salad among four plates. Garnish with croutons and cheese, if desired.

PROVINCE

161 North Jefferson Street, West Loop
(312) 669-9900
http://chicago.provincerestaurant.com
Chef-Owner: Randy Zweiban

When Randy Zweiban opened up shop in this LEED-Gold certified building (the highest "green" building ranking by the government-sponsored Leadership in Energy and Environmental Design) after spending a decade heading up the kitchen at the longtime River North institution Nacional 27, it was the perfect "green" fit. Zweiban has focused on sourcing locally since his early days as the right-hand chef for Nuevo Latino grandfather Norman Van Aken in Miami, and later at the popular Lettuce Entertain You restaurant. At Province, he's made local farms the star of the show, set against the backdrop of energy- and water-efficiency and an airy dining room bright with natural light, bold pink, red, and blue accents, stainless steel, and lots of clean, modern lines.

Just as the "small plates" phase began to grow old, Zweiban invented an even better menu concept—printed on recycled paper and clipped onto a brightly colored, toxin-free, recycled-vinyl board, of course. His selection of small, big, bigger, and biggest portions allows guests to pick and choose among a wide variety of flavors and textures. "I wanted to give people the opportunity to design their own progressive menu instead of having to lock into just one appetizer or just one entree," he says.

The name Province reflects the various "regions" of Spain, Mexico, and South America from which the menu is drawn, all while using foods from family farms in Illinois, Indiana, Wisconsin, and Michigan. Zweiban's famous for hosting farmers for special dinners, and

he's regularly seen loading his cart at the city's farmers' markets. Even the restaurant's elaborate cocktail program, headed up by mixologist Jeff Donahue, showcases artisanal spirits with garnishes made from the bounty of the Midwest. Here Zweiban dresses up a classic Mexican tortilla soup with a confit of free-range pastured chicken from an Indiana farm and a puree of locally grown red onions, peppers, and garlic.

TORTILLA SOUP WITH SHREDDED CHICKEN AND AVOCADO RELISH
(Serves 8)

3 chicken legs
3 chicken thighs
Kosher salt and freshly ground black pepper,
    to taste
6 cups canola oil, divided
6 white corn tortillas, cut into ¼-inch strips
1 cup diced red onion
6 tomatillos, diced
4 cloves garlic, chopped
1 serrano chile, stemmed, seeded, and minced
3 medium red peppers, stemmed, seeded,
    and chopped
2 quarts vegetable broth or stock

For the avocado relish:

1 ripe Haas avocado, peeled, pitted, and
    finely diced
1 tablespoon minced red onion
1 tablespoon freshly squeezed lime juice
1 teaspoon chopped fresh cilantro
Kosher salt and freshly ground black pepper,
    to taste

Preheat oven to 350°F. Season chicken with salt and pepper. Heat two tablespoons of the oil in a large sauté pan over medium-high heat. Sauté chicken until nicely browned, about 2–3 minutes per side. Remove from pan, set aside.

Add remaining oil to the pan and heat to 175°F, checking the temperature with a thermometer. Return chicken to pan and cover with lid or heavy-duty foil.

Roast in oven for 35–40 minutes or until meat is fork-tender. Remove chicken from pan, reserving the oil. When chicken is cool enough to handle, shred, discarding skin and bones.

Heat the oil back up to 325°F. Fry the tortilla strips until crispy, about 1–2 minutes. Drain the strips on paper towels. Pour off all but one-quarter of the oil.

Heat the remaining oil over medium heat. Sauté the onion, tomatillos, garlic, and chile until lightly browned, about 5 minutes. Add the peppers, broth, and all but 1 cup of the crispy tortillas.

Simmer the soup until the peppers are soft, about 10 minutes. Puree in a high-speed blender or using an immersion blender.

In a small bowl, combine avocado, onion, lime juice, and cilantro. Season with salt and pepper.

To serve, divide shredded chicken evenly among eight shallow bowls. Pour in soup. Top with avocado relish and crispy tortillas.

North Pond

2610 North Cannon Drive, Lincoln Park
(773) 477-5845
www.northpondrestaurant.com
Chef-Owner: Bruce Sherman

Once a warming house for ice-skaters on the pond at the north end of grassy Lincoln Park, the quaint stone building that is North Pond Restaurant has been providing a quiet refuge amid the bustling urban jungle for more than a decade. Surrounded by green grass, leafy trees, and clucking ducks in the warmer months and with fluffy white snow and softly trolling geese in the winter, it's no surprise that the intimate restaurant sits just a couple hundred yards from the Peggy Notebaert Nature Museum, where Green City Market moves its farmers indoors during the winter.

It's also fitting for chef Bruce Sherman, a longtime advocate of the city's largest farmers' market and considered one of the founders of the local farm movement in Chicago. Sherman serves as board chairman for Chef's Collaborative, an organization of chefs and other food professionals working together to promote local, seasonal food and to advocate on other social and sustainable food issues.

Sherman is like a watchtower guard who won't leave his post. Quiet and collected, focused and firm, he stands night after night at the expediting spot along the exposed kitchen line, occasionally moving behind the plating area to work with his young chefs in training. A mentor for countless rising stars in the city, Sherman is as institutional to Chicago as is his restaurant and the peaceful pond that is its namesake. Here he offers up a dish that, in its simplicity, showcases the best of the seasonal Midwestern bounty—sweet corn, farm-fresh eggs, smoky bacon, and candy-like onions—with the sophistication in cooking technique and plate presentation reflective of North Pond's fine-dining yet approachable cuisine.

Poached Farm Eggs with Corn Pancakes and Maui Onion Pipérade
(Serves 6)

For the corn pancakes:

1 cup all-purpose flour
1 1/3 cups yellow cornmeal
1 tablespoon baking powder
½ teaspoon baking soda
½ teaspoon salt, plus extra for seasoning
¼ teaspoon white pepper, plus extra for seasoning
2 eggs
2/3 cup buttermilk
¼ cup honey
1 tablespoon roasted garlic
3 tablespoons vegetable oil

3 ears corn, grilled, kernels cut off and sautéed (optional)

For the pipérade:

1 tablespoon olive oil
1 small Vidalia or other sweet onion, diced (about ¼ cup)
Pinch of salt and white pepper
2 red bell peppers, roasted, skinned, seeded, and diced
1 clove garlic, peeled and crushed
Pinch of sugar

1 tablespoon water
2 plum tomatoes, peeled, seeded, and chopped
1 tablespoon balsamic vinegar
3 tablespoons cold butter, cubed

For the poached eggs and garnish:

½ cup distilled white vinegar
3 cups water
6 farm-fresh eggs (preferably organic or local,
    purchased within last 5 days)
1 tablespoon oil or unsalted butter
1 tablespoon each chopped fresh chives and
    parsley
Tabasco or other hot pepper sauce
6–12 slices smoked bacon, cooked until crisp,
    for garnish

First, prepare the pancakes. Combine the flour, cornmeal, baking powder, baking soda, ½ teaspoon salt, and white pepper in a large bowl and mix gently. In a separate bowl, whisk together the eggs, buttermilk, honey, roasted garlic, and oil.

Make a well in the center of the dry ingredients. Pour in half of the wet mixture and whisk to incorporate. Whisk in the rest of the wet mixture. Batter should be coarse and slightly thick but not runny. Add additional buttermilk or flour if batter is too dry or runny. Fold in the optional corn. Cover and chill batter for at least 1 hour, or up to a day ahead.

To prepare the pipérade, heat the oil in a large skillet over medium heat and sauté the diced onions until soft and translucent, about 2–3 minutes. Season with a pinch of salt and white pepper. Add the peppers, garlic, sugar, and water, stirring to combine. Continue to cook until fragrant, about 2–3 minutes. Stir in the tomatoes and balsamic vinegar. Cover and simmer, about 10 minutes. Remove cover and continue to simmer until liquid is reduced to a tablespoon, about 5 minutes. Remove from heat and cool

slightly. Stir in butter and reserve. (This can be made a day ahead.)

Bring the water and vinegar to a boil in a medium saucepan. Crack the eggs into separate ramekins or small bowls. Turn heat down to a gentle simmer and, one by one, slip eggs into the water. Poach eggs until the white is set at the thickest part and the yolk is still runny, about 2½–3½ minutes. Remove from water and reserve.

Meanwhile, preheat a cast-iron or other heavy pan over medium heat. Add oil or butter and, when hot, drop heaping spoonfuls of the corn batter in three places in the pan, flattening each slightly with a spatula. Cook pancakes until golden on both sides, about 4–5 minutes. Place pancakes on separate plates. Repeat to make six total pancakes.

Top each pancake evenly with the pipérade, chopped herbs, and a dash of Tabasco or hot pepper sauce. Carefully place a poached egg atop each pancake. Garnish with crisp bacon.

CHICAGO'S GREEN CITY MARKET
AND LOCAL FOOD MOVEMENT

The sun has just started to peek above the placid shoreline, splashing the sky purple and pink. A half mile west of the sandy Lake Michigan beach on the lawn of Lincoln Park, the sounds of carts squeaking, tents being pitched, and banners unfurling break through the early Saturday morning silence.

A few dedicated shoppers have already arrived, baskets and cloth bags in hand, ready to jump at the day's first pick. Then come the chefs, their wagons loaded with empty crates ready for harvesting.

April and May bring the first out of the earth—baby asparagus cut gently from the ground, big globes of fragrant garlic and just as fragrant ramps, tender arugula, and micro greens. By June the first few candy-sweet strawberries have arrived. And in July and August, the heart of the Midwestern harvest season, big wooden bowls spill over with plump red, yellow, purple, and green-striped tomatoes, flanked by rows of bright yellow ears of sweet corn and bushels of chard, spinach, mustard greens, and herbs. Come fall, you'll find earthy red and gold beets, barrels of squash, baby potatoes in browns, blues, and purples, and the popular Honey Crisp apples, tart and strong like cider. Then there are the rich cheeses and hand-churned butter, the humanely raised beef, pork, and lamb, the whole grains and legumes, the fresh-baked breads and pastries, the sweet homemade pies. And the fruit smoothies—oh, the smoothies.

This is Green City Market (GCM), Chicago's largest outdoor farmers' market.

This is Abby Mandel's dream come true.

"Abby had a vision for this city," says Sarah Stegner, longtime friend, GCM founding board member, and chef-owner of Prairie Grass Café. "Abby imagined a market that would increase the flow of local foods to the Chicago table, and she's done that. She's made it that much more accessible to the people and to the chefs of this city to go down the street and not only buy local, fresh produce, but also connect with the farmers."

What started in 1999 with just five farms and a few makeshift tents in a dark street alley has grown to a full-fledged operation in Chicago's largest park with more than fifty farms and local food purveyors, a full-time staff and troop of volunteers, an advisory board, cooking demonstrations by local chefs, live music, kids' activities, educational sessions, lunchtime crepes, herb-aioli-topped burgers, and an annual chef's barbecue featuring almost a hundred local culinarians, among other fundraising events. Just after the market's tenth anniversary, Abby Mandel passed away after a battle with cancer, but her legend and vision lives on.

Since her death, the market has also grown to remain open almost year-round. When it's warm, or warmer, the market opens up outside from May through October. During the winter, it moves inside to the Peggy Notebaert Nature Museum just down the street, closing only for a few weeks during the icy grip of Chicago's winter in January and February.

For many farmers in Illinois, Wisconsin, Michigan, and Indiana, this is the primary source of business—a place where they can also connect with chefs to boost their revenue. Now, with such a widespread dedication to Slow Food and eating locally, the number of chefs and cooks who shop here almost rivals the number of city residents flocking to the stands.

Mandel spent many hours working with former longtime mayor Richard M. Daley and local aldermen to support the local food economy and develop laws, or relax them, in order to help Green City Market and its farmers grow and flourish. A close friend of Alice Waters, Mandel also called upon local chef friends Stegner, Bruce Sherman of North Pond, Carrie Nahabedian of Naha, and others to develop the first board for the nonprofit operation, whose founding members to this day continue to advise on GCM-related initiatives and decisions, not to mention shopping regularly at the market themselves.

GCM has also served as a source of inspiration for other farmers' markets opening up around the city, from pockets of stands downtown at the Daley Center and Federal Building to larger markets up north in the neighborhoods of Logan Square, Lincoln Square, Andersonville, and Wicker Park. And with the growth of the Slow Food movement around the country and in Chicago since the middle of the last decade, countless chefs, food retailers, caterers, and others draw upon the best of the Midwestern bounty these markets bring.

Perhaps the most vivid memory Stegner and others share of Mandel is a photo shown round the country at the time of her death. Mandel is standing in the middle of the market holding a big bundle of long-stemmed pink flowers, a cloth bag slung over one arm brimming with curly green carrot tops, fresh herbs, and a big elephant ear of glossy rainbow chard. She is the epitome of the Slow Food philosophy then and now—the idea that we should return to our roots, literally, celebrating the foods that nourish our bodies, our souls, and the earth. Especially our local earths, wherever those may be.

Elate

Hotel Felix
111 West Huron Street, River North
(312) 202-9900
www.elatechicago.com
Executive Chef: Chris Curren

Tucked inside Chicago's first LEED-certified hotel, Elate at the boutique Hotel Felix boasts sustainability, from the reclaimed wood tables and low-wattage lighting to the local farm-grown spinach on its menu. LEED (Leadership in Energy and Environmental Design) challenges new building projects to reduce their energy and water consumption, use reusable and recyclable materials during construction, and subscribe to a battery of other guidelines for creating sustainable spaces in order to earn credits toward various levels of "green" building certification.

Dark and geometric, but softened by the candlelit tables and sharable, prettily presented plates, Elate gives off the same intimate feel you might find in a cozy cocktail lounge from the 1920s or '30s. Retro and modern at the same time, classic meets creative here, both in cocktail artistry and in the simple but elegant dishes created by Chris Curren, chef-owner of Blue 13 who moved over as consulting executive chef upon former chef Randal Jacobs's departure.

Seasons and sustainability are what drive restaurateur Anthony Fiore's boutique lounge in a quintessential boutique hotel, but Curren's menu also shows flavor influences from around the globe. Spinach skewers, developed by Jacobs's drawing upon Colombian and even Scottish cuisines (breaded Scotch-like eggs), are built with a farmers'-market-driven ingredient list—a foundation upon which Curren has continued the local and Midwestern farm focus.

Spinach Salad Skewers with Chicharrones, Molten Eggs, and Crème
(Serves 4)

For the spinach skewers:

4 10-inch wooden skewers
1 pound baby spinach, rinsed clean and dried
8 frisée lettuce leaves, rinsed clean and dried

For the vinaigrette:

1 small shallot, minced
3 spears chives, minced
2 tablespoons sherry vinegar
6 tablespoons grapeseed oil
Salt and pepper

For the crème:

3 ounces crème fraîche
2 tablespoons buttermilk
1/8 teaspoon white truffle oil
1/4 teaspoon kosher salt
1/4 freshly ground black pepper

For the chicharrones*:

½ pound pork skin (from a local butcher),
    cut into 2-inch-thick strips
Vegetable oil, for frying

For the "molten" eggs:

3 quarts water
2 tablespoons distilled white vinegar
5 organic and/or free-range eggs, divided
½ cup all-purpose flour
Salt and pepper
½ cup panko breadcrumbs
Pinch of smoked paprika

Using one of the wooden skewers, pierce baby spinach leaves though their center until a 1-inch-thick stack is formed. Add to the skewer one piece of torn frisée pierced through the white portion, then repeat the layering process until you have three 1-inch spinach stacks separated by the frisée. Repeat with remaining skewers, removing the spinach stems with scissors.

To make the vinaigrette, cover the shallot and chives with sherry vinegar and let sit for 15 minutes to allow flavors to macerate. Whisk in grapeseed oil, salt, and pepper. Refrigerate until serving. (This can be made up to a day ahead.)

For the crème, in a small bowl whisk together the crème fraîche, buttermilk, white truffle oil, salt, and pepper. Refrigerate until serving.

To make the molten eggs, bring the water and vinegar to a boil. Meanwhile, prepare an ice bath. Gently place 4 eggs, in their shells, in the boiling water for 5 minutes 20 seconds. Remove and plunge into the ice bath. Once cool enough to handle, peel the eggs.

Set out three small, shallow bowls. In one, beat the remaining egg. In another, gently mix together the flour, salt, and pepper. In the third, place the panko. Dredge each semi-hard-boiled egg first in the flour mixture, then in the beaten egg, and lastly in the panko.

To fry the chicharrones, pour vegetable oil into a deep frying pan or pot to a depth of 2 inches. Heat the oil over medium-high heat for about 5 minutes, or to 350°F. Add the pork skins. As each chicharrón becomes puffed and golden, remove and drain on paper towels. Set oil aside for later use.

Next, fry the molten eggs. Making sure the oil is at 350°F, drop in the dredged eggs, and fry for about 45 seconds, or until crispy. Drain on paper towels.

To serve, gently toss the 4 skewers in a bowl with just enough sherry vinaigrette so the leaves are lightly coated but not wilted or weighed down. In a serving bowl, smear a dollop of the crème along the bottom. Dust lightly with paprika. Lay skewers in the crème-lined bowl and place the eggs and chicharrones alongside. For an alternative presentation, serve each guest 1 skewer, 1 egg, and a handful of the chicharrones in an individual crème-lined bowl. Serve with sharp knives for cutting the egg.

*Note: Chicharrones, or fried pork skins, are a traditional snack in Colombia and other South American countries, as well as in parts of Mexico. The skins are cut into bite-size pieces and deep-fried until they puff up. Some chefs fry the skins, dehydrate them in a slow oven overnight, and then fry them again the next day so they become light and puffy. Chicharrones are also available as a packaged good at Hispanic food markets and other specialty grocery stores. When making homemade chicharrones, ask your local butcher for pork skin. If it is not already cut up, make sure you use a sharp knife, as the skin has a leathery, tough texture. Always let the frying oil heat up adequately before dropping in the skins, about 5 minutes or more depending on the amount used.

Bistronomic

840 N. Wabash Avenue, Gold Coast
(312) 944-8400
www.bistronomic.net
Owners: Matt Fisher and John Ward
Executive Chef: Martial Noguier

Martial Noguier left his long-held post at fine-dining Café des Architectes in the upscale Sofitel Hotel to open this first place of his own. Essentially a scaled-down, more charming version of Café des Architectes, the classic-meets-modern bistro offers the same French classics like pâtés, terrines, and cheeses, but takes a more rustic approach to entrees. At Café des Architectes, Noguier had definitively secured his reputation for outstanding cookery and service, building upon his previous achievements, which once included head chef at one sixtyblue.

Noguier is also known for effortlessly blending the sweet with the savory in a lightened up, contemporary French style with some American influences. His choice of peekytoe crab in a delicate salad with American apple and French frisée clearly reflects the grace, style, and technique that is Martial.

Peekytoe Crab with Apple-Frisée Salad and Apple Jelly

(Serves 4)

For the apple jelly:

1 cup apple juice
1 teaspoon unflavored gelatin
Juice of ½ lime
½ tablespoon apple cider vinegar
Pinch each of sea salt and freshly ground
    black pepper
2 tablespoons chopped fresh chives, divided

For the apple-frisée salad and vinaigrette:

2 tablespoons lemon juice
1 teaspoon minced shallot
½ teaspoon honey
2 tablespoons vegetable oil
¼ teaspoon sea salt
¼ teaspoon freshly ground black pepper
2 cups chopped frisée lettuce leaves
1 small apple, cut into julienne strips

For the crab and garnish:

8 ounces peekytoe crabmeat, or other
    good-quality lump crabmeat
Zest of 1 lemon
4 basil leaves, rolled together and thinly sliced
4 tablespoons puree of drained, jarred, or
    canned piquillo peppers
2 breakfast radishes, thinly sliced
8 dried apple slices
1 lime, cut into 8 segments

First, prepare the apple jelly. Combine the apple juice and gelatin powder in a small bowl. Let stand 5 minutes. Add the lime juice, apple cider vinegar, salt, and pepper, stirring together over an ice bath until the mixture is thickened and coats the back of a spoon. Stir in 1 teaspoon of the chopped chives, cover, and chill in the refrigerator completely, about 1 hour. (Can be prepared a day ahead.)

For the vinaigrette, whisk together the lemon juice, shallot, and honey. Pour in vegetable oil, whisking constantly. Season with salt and pepper.

Toss together the crab, 4 teaspoons of the chives, the lemon zest, basil, and 3 tablespoons of the lemon vinaigrette. In a separate bowl, toss the frisée with the apple, remaining vinaigrette, and remaining teaspoon of chives.

To plate, spoon or brush a small amount of the pureed piquillo peppers on each of four plates. Set two radish slices over the puree and top with a quarter of the crab mixture. Place two additional radish slices atop the crab. Spoon about 1 teaspoon of the apple jelly around the radish slices. Top each plate evenly with the apple-frisée mixture. Garnish with apple chips and lime segments.

GREEN ZEBRA

1460 WEST CHICAGO AVENUE, WEST TOWN
(312) 243-7100
WWW.GREENZEBRACHICAGO.COM
OWNER–EXECUTIVE CHEF: SHAWN MCCLAIN

It's hard not to think of Shawn McClain and the word "vegetarian" at the same time. Though McClain's not one, he's credited by national food critics as a pioneer, elevating vegetarian cuisine to a modern and creative fine-dining level, not unlike Alice Waters out West. The difference is, McClain introduced this cuisine in the heart of the meat-loving Midwest, at a time when vegetarianism was by no means as cool as it is now.

A native of San Diego and a graduate of local Kendall College, McClain first rose to chef stardom at the legendary Trio, where Grant Achatz later joined the ranks. For seven years at Trio he honed his experimental, contemporary-creative, ultrarefined style and began what would be a decade-long trailblazing foray into both meat and meatless cuisine. When McClain left in 2001 to open Spring, a seafood-focused restaurant, that same year the restaurant earned a nomination for best new restaurant by the James Beard Foundation, and one year later McClain was named *Esquire* magazine's Chef of the Year. The restaurant closed in 2010 after almost a decade, a stretch that saw the artsy Wicker Park neighborhood emerge from tougher, rougher times as one of the most culturally diverse, popular places to live in the city.

In 2004, when McClain opened his second outpost, Green Zebra, now his signature restaurant, he raised some eyebrows with haute cuisine that excluded animal protein. First came the true vegetarians and West Coast transplants. Then, one by one, more followed and created a cult clientele. It wasn't long before the rest of the country caught on. Nowadays, a heightened awareness about how our food is produced and the subsequent impact on the environment has turned many of us into this type of "flexitarian" eater—embracing

of vegetarianism, concerned about the sustainability of seafood, and appreciative of meat as a special treat that should be proffered as such. Turns out McClain knew what he was doing a long time ago.

Most recently, McClain has split his time with Las Vegas, where he was recruited to open up shop at the multibillion-dollar CityCenter complex of casino hotels and restaurants. His concept Sage, at the Aria Hotel, continues his New American saga with even more refinement and scale, from the cooking to the plating. And he still makes time to train and mentor younger, up-and-coming chefs as he always has. With this delicate salad using crystal-thin Japanese somen noodles, McClain demonstrates the trademark East-meets-West style he first honed at Trio.

Somen Noodle Salad with Pickled Papaya and Edamame Puree

(Serves 6)

For the ginger-soy dressing:

2 tablespoons minced fresh ginger
½ teaspoon minced garlic
¼ teaspoon Chinese mustard powder
1 tablespoon palm sugar
1/3 cup soy sauce
1 tablespoon sake
1 tablespoon mirin
½ cup grapeseed oil
2 teaspoons sesame oil

For the pickled papaya:

2 cups rice vinegar
1 cup water
1 clove garlic, peeled and crushed
1 tablespoon thinly sliced fresh ginger
2 stalks fresh lemongrass, pounded and
    coarsely chopped
¼ cup sugar
1 teaspoon sea salt
1 large fresh green papaya (unripened),
    peeled, cut into thin ribbons (2 cups)

For the edamame puree and the salad:

2 cups edamame beans, shelled, cooked, divided
¼ cup water
Sea salt, to taste
3 cups cooked somen noodles, cooled and lightly
    tossed in oil
6 ounces fresh hearts of palm (about one 6-inch
    stalk), thinly sliced (may substitute canned
    hearts of palm, drained)
1 cup Chinese long beans, blanched, cut into
    2-inch pieces
6 ounces fresh mustard greens

Pinch of sea salt

To prepare the ginger soy dressing, combine ginger, garlic, mustard powder, palm sugar, soy sauce, sake, and mirin in a small bowl. Whisk together vigorously and let stand 15 minutes to develop flavors. Whisk in grapeseed and sesame oils; set aside.

For the pickled green papaya, in a small nonreactive saucepan, combine vinegar, water, garlic, ginger, lemongrass, sugar, and salt and bring to a simmer. Remove from heat and let stand 20 minutes or until sugar and salt have dissolved. Strain through a fine strainer and return to a simmer. Remove from heat and add papaya. Place in a small bowl over ice to cool. Allow papaya to rest in pickling liquid at least 2 hours or overnight.

For the edamame puree, combine 1 cup of the edamame in a high-speed blender or food processor with ¼ cup water. Puree until smooth, scraping down sides often. Season to taste with sea salt.

In a large mixing bowl, combine the somen noodles, hearts of palm, Chinese long beans, and remaining 1 cup edamame beans. Drain pickled papaya and add to bowl. Add 2 tablespoons of the dressing and toss to coat. If salad is still dry, add more dressing by the teaspoon, to taste. Add torn mustard greens and a pinch of sea salt; toss gently. To plate, spoon edamame puree onto six chilled serving plates or bowls and spread with the back of a spoon. Top with noodle salad and serve.

A book about Chicago chefs would be incomplete without mentioning the handful of schools that have produced so many of the city's successful culinarians. Kendall College, in particular, has seen countless graduates go on to build successful, even legendary culinary careers throughout the country and particularly in Chicago—Shawn McClain of Green Zebra (page 16), Mindy Segal of Mindy's Hot Chocolate (page 170), Jose Garces of Mercat a la Planxa (page 106), Todd Stein of The Florentine (page 46), Nick Lacasse of The Drawing Room (page 96), and many others. Peggy Ryan, the former owner and chef of the acclaimed Va Pensiero in Evanston, has returned to Kendall as a chef-instructor, earning the Women Chefs & Restaurateurs' highest honor as Educator of the Year in 2009.

Shawn McClain and Mindy Segal have remained particularly active in mentoring all up-and-coming chefs, including many fellow Kendall graduates. Nick Lacasse, for example, trained under McClain for years before putting his current restaurant on the Chicago culinary map.

"I think what Kendall combines are really the key parts of the great recipe for success," says Chris Koetke, vice president of Laureate International Universities, which bought out Kendall in 2008 and has since promoted Koetke from dean of the school of culinary arts to his current role. "It's history—we've been doing this for twenty-five-plus years—it's a commitment to excellence in education, which is what I call an intense education with very high standards. And then to round it out, you have a truly gifted faculty with generous real-world food-service and managerial experience, combined with a great facility that's world class by anybody's measure."

Kendall started its culinary arts program in 1985. Originally located in Evanston, the college moved in 2005 to the West Town area near downtown Chicago into completely revamped quarters in a former production facility for Sara Lee, which also donated materials and equipment for a few of the school's new kitchens. The new facility included the Dining Room, a white-tablecloth, fine-dining teaching restaurant open to the public, serving contemporary American dishes in a clean, bright space surrounded by windows with skyline views. In 2009 Kendall launched an ambitious project to build a completely new kitchen for the Dining Room in a former catering space at the back of the dining room that often went unused.

The multimillion-dollar project and Koetke's "kitchen of my dreams" included all new energy-efficient equipment combined with natural and CFL lighting, a state-of-the-art heating and ventilation system, water-saving sink accessories, and an expertly designed kitchen layout to realize energy and water savings. The "green," environmentally friendly kitchen is in line with Kendall's recent positioning as a leader in sustainable education among culinary schools across the country. That move was kicked off by an elaborate schoolwide recycling and composting program to cut down on food waste and to produce enriched soil, not only for local farms, but also for the school's chef's garden where students learn basic farming skills and grow food for their own use.

"Sustainability education has been something that we have been leading for the last six-plus years," Koetke says. "The way we've led is by, first of all, being an example to our students. We teach sustainability from the very beginning of the curriculum to the end. The next step which has made it really powerful was taking this beyond Kendall College to teach the larger community." That has included partnering with the National Restaurant Association's Conserve initiative.

Headed by chef-instructor Benjamin Browning, a veteran executive chef formerly with the Boka Restaurant Group, the Dining Room earned a prestigious mention in 2010 in the first U.S. edition of the *Michelin Guide,* an achievement made possible by both the kitchen and front-of-the-house staff including servers and management.

But it's not fair to spotlight Kendall without naming the other culinary schools in Chicago that have produced successful chefs, from the Cooking and Hospitality Institute of Chicago (CHIC) (recently bought out by Le Cordon Bleu) from which former, longtime Topolobampo/Frontera Grill chef de cuisine and Rick Bayless right-hand man Brian Enyart graduated, to the Illinois Institute of Art and Washburne Culinary Institute on the South Side, one of the oldest culinary schools in the country, which donates thousands of dollars in scholarship awards to aspiring chefs and which runs the acclaimed Parrot Cage teaching restaurant at the beautiful South Shore Cultural Center along Jackson Harbor. Meg Galus, formerly of Café des Architectes (page 185), now at NoMI Kitchen, earned her diploma from the French Pastry School in Chicago.

Socca / Redd Herring

Socca
3301 North Clark Street, Lakeview
(773) 248-1155
www.soccachicago.com

Redd Herring
31 South Prospect Avenue, Clarendon Hills
(630) 908-7295
www.redd-herring.com
Owner–Executive Chef: Roger Herring

When people say "neighborhood restaurant," some think of Cheers. Others think of a local wine bar or pizza joint. In Chicago, Lakeview neighborhood-ites think of Socca.

Not a French bistro, but not a pasta-heavy Italian restaurant either, it gently merges the two cultures in chef-owner Roger Herring's modern spin on Mediterranean cuisine, pairing Italian risotto with French-style braised meats and Italian polenta with scallops in a very French leek-based broth. Socca takes its name from the southeastern French crepe made with chickpea flour, olive oil, and lots of crushed black pepper.

Herring has a sweet, almost surferlike California appeal. With semi-long, curly blond locks, he talks a little slower, listens a little louder, smiles a lot sunnier, and generally understands the meaning of laid-back. But his day-in, day-out hard work ethic has helped him stay in business over the last decade, even seeing him through a major economic recession, and now he's got a second spot, Redd Herring, a modern chophouse in the northwest suburbs.

Socca's core of regulars is so strong that, when Herring once tried to take the famed rabbit risotto off the menu, he was met with a staunch outcry. His regulars even include out-of-town business travelers who've escaped the downtown area and come back often. These days, Herring simply tweaks the old favorites to include more seasonal ingredients, and he's expanded the appetizer list with more sharable mix-and-match items.

One such appetizer that's led the roster since day one is his pizzette, featured once on the Food Network. Herring switches up the toppings from time to time, but fans and local media say he started the "flatbread" trend long before that word existed. When he makes the dough, Herring adds any that's left over from the previous day's batch to develop a more sourdough taste and texture. He also refrigerates the dough for at least 24 to 36 hours before use. While the recipe below doesn't call for those procedures, it is possible to make the dough ahead of time, freezing the extra dough balls for later use. (If you've already done this, simply thaw one of the premade 3½-inch dough balls and go straight to step 4.) In the summertime, cook pizzette on an oiled grill for a charred, smoky flavor.

Pizzette with Caramelized Onions, Fennel Sausage, and Gorgonzola

(Makes one 10 x 13-inch flatbread, plus extra dough)

For the dough:

½ ounce yeast
1⅓ cups warm water (110°F)
2 tablespoons honey
⅓ cup olive oil
3⅔ cups all-purpose flour, plus more for kneading
1 cup whole wheat flour
½ teaspoon salt

For the topping:

1 medium sweet yellow onion,
　　cut into ½-inch slices
1 tablespoon unsalted butter
1 tablespoon plus 1 teaspoon olive oil, divided
½ pound fennel sausage
1 cup crimini mushrooms, sliced
¼ cup crumbled Gorgonzola cheese
Freshly grated Parmesan cheese

For the dough, in a small bowl combine the yeast, water, honey, and oil and let sit 15 minutes to bloom the yeast. Pour the mixture into an electric stand mixer fitted with the paddle attachment. Add both flours and salt and mix on medium speed until elastic, about 3–4 minutes. If dough is too sticky, add more all-purpose flour, 1 tablespoon at a time, until dough becomes smooth and elastic.

Transfer dough to a counter or chopping board, cover with plastic wrap and a cloth towel, and allow dough to rise, about 2 hours.

Remove covers and punch down dough. Cut dough into 3 pieces of ½ ounce each, rolling each piece into a ball and setting on a sheet tray. Cover tray lightly with plastic wrap and let rise another 20 minutes. Refrigerate for at least 1–2 hours, up to overnight.

Meanwhile, prepare the topping. In a medium sauté pan over medium heat, cook onions in butter and 1 tablespoon oil until soft and lightly browned, about 5 minutes. Add sausage and cook until sausage is browned and onions caramelized, about another 5 minutes. Remove mixture from pan and add remaining teaspoon oil. Cook mushrooms over medium heat until they are browned and juices have evaporated, about 7 minutes.

Heat the oven to 500°F. Roll out dough on a lightly floured surface into a rectangle about 10 x 13 inches and ½ inch thick, and place on a lightly oiled baking sheet. Freeze the remaining dough balls for later use. Brush dough with olive oil and top evenly with the Gorgonzola cheese. Add mushrooms, and then the onion-sausage mixture. Sprinkle with Parmesan cheese.

Bake pizzette for 10–15 minutes, or until crust is crispy, edges are golden and Parmesan cheese is lightly browned. Transfer to a wooden board, cut into squares, and serve on the board for a rustic presentation and to maintain a crispy bottom.

Chicago's known for many things—the wind, shopping along Mag Mile, the skyscrapers, snowy winters, and hot humid summers at the beach. It's also a rich food-lover's dream, from the char-grilled burgers and ballpark dogs to stuffed burritos, Italian beef sandwiches, caramel popcorn, and, of course, deep dish pizza.

Ultra-thick, stringy cheese, sweet tomato sauce, butter crust, the occasional fennel-spiked sausage. Deep dish pizza, a stringent departure from the thinner, chewier-crusted pizza found in New York, was born at Pizzeria Uno on Ohio Street in the 1940s after owner Ric Riccardo looked for something heartier to serve Chicagoans than the traditional thin-crust version. But Riccardo is not credited with the pie's actual invention—historians still debate whether it was Riccardo, who died in the 1950s, his business partner Ike Sewell, or Rudy Malnati, then the manager, who later went on to open Pizzeria Due across the street. That later led to another famous deep dish pizza chain in the Malnati family, Lou Malnati's. And then there's also Pizano's from the same family. Now deep dish joints in Chicago run the gamut from Gino's to Giordano's, Pequod's to Renaldi's, Aurelio's to Edwardo's, and the list goes on.

Described as a cheese casserole in a cast-iron pan, Uno's and Malnati's especially have been able to achieve that crackly, slightly caramelized crunch from the buttery shortbread crust thanks to seasoned pans (which don't see much soap and water) and double-stacked, superhot ovens. Sausage is the most popular, but pepperoni, spinach, and plain old cheese are steady standbys. Tableside, most Chicagoans sprinkle their slice (or slices) with oregano, Parmesan cheese, and red pepper flakes.

Many restaurateurs and chefs have chosen to escape the heaviness of deep dish, producing pizzas that go back to their Italian roots. The pies have the doughier, chewier crusts commonly found in Rome and Naples, and are charred in wood-burning or even coal-fired ovens. Great Lake Pizza and Spacca Napoli on the North Side have won accolades, while downtown La Madia, Osteria Via Stato, Quartino, and Coalfire continue to draw the crowds. In the urban-hip Wicker Park neigborhood, Piece, a popular brewery/pizzeria owned by New Haven native Bill Jacobs, features pies from his hometown. These have a semi-thin, chewy crust similar to a Neapolitan pizza, but topped with grated pecorino Romano or Parmesan cheese instead of mozzarella. Nearby in Bucktown the certified organic restaurant Crust, by Michael Altenberg, chef-owner of the local-seasonal institution Bistro Campagne, serves slices topped with Wisconsin cheeses and locally grown vegetables alongside fruity cocktails.

Carnivale

702 West Fulton Market, Fulton Market
(312) 850-5005
WWW.CARNIVALECHICAGO.COM
Owner-Proprietor: Jerry Kleiner
Executive Chef: David Dworshak

Walking into Carnivale is like walking into a Brazilian churrascaria with Las Vegas glitz. The main dining room, a 300-seat, 4,000-square-foot warehouse of a space features lofty ceilings and walls lined with wine bottles. In fact, servers have to use ladders just to get the top-shelf picks.

It's this rainbow of bold fuchsias, magentas, rich reds, and pungent oranges, the eclectic mishmash of fabrics and textures, and the extravagance that has shaped legendary Chicago restaurateur Jerry Kleiner's reputation for all things glitz and glamour. In an established portfolio that includes Red Light (brought to fame by former chef Jackie Shen), Opera, the now-closed Marché, and newcomer 33 Club, middle child Carnivale started off in similar fashion—as a place to see and be seen—but has grown into more of an event and drinks-and-apps destination, thanks to its loud and lively front bar and upstairs private space with seating for an additional 300. Photos of famous actors and models line the walls throughout the restaurant and even in the bathrooms, another Kleiner trademark.

The name Carnivale may stand for the eclectic décor but also for the menu—an ensemble of flavors from Mexico and Central and South America, such as big bowls of fresh-made guacamole, braised pork shoulder, plantains, masa, black beans, lime, cilantro, and jicama. And, like many Chicago restaurants, this one too has focused on local, seasonal produce. Mark Mendez, formerly the executive chef, incorporated many sustainable practices in running the restaurant, including building a rooftop garden. He also mentored former sous-chef David Dworshak, who has since taken the lead.

Dworshak's arepa recipe falls in line with the traditional Colombian version—flatter, browned on a griddle, and often accompanying pork belly and plantains, but with influences from the Argentinean version incorporating cheese in the mix.

STUFFED COLOMBIAN AREPAS WITH BERKSHIRE PORK BELLY, PLANTAIN, BLACK BEANS, AND JICAMA

(Serves 6)

For the Berkshire pork belly:

1–2 ounces salt
1 tablespoon freshly ground black pepper
1–2 ounces brown sugar
1 teaspoon ground coriander
1 teaspoon cayenne pepper
1 teaspoon dried oregano
1 pound pork belly

For the arepa:

2 cups masarepa flour *
2 cups hot water
2 tablespoons lard or butter
Salt and pepper, to taste

For the avocado puree:

2 ripe avocadoes, peeled, pitted, and diced
2 tablespoons fresh lime juice
1 tablespoon sautéed minced garlic
1 tablespoon chopped cilantro
1 serrano chile, minced
Salt and pepper, to taste

For the stuffing:

1 cup fried sweet plantains (packaged or
    freshly made)
1 cup canned black beans, drained and rinsed
1 cup queso Cotija or Monterey Jack cheese,
    shredded, or crumbled queso fresco
1 clove minced garlic
1 fresh jicama, peeled and sliced into
    1-inch-long pieces
Hot sauce

In a small bowl, mix together all the dry ingredients for the pork belly and rub thoroughly over the meat. Wrap and refrigerate for at least 1–2 hours, up to three days.

Heat the oven to 425°F. Roast pork belly, fat side up, until browned, about 20 minutes. Reduce oven temperature to 300°F and continue to roast pork until fork tender, about 1 hour. Set aside.

Combine all ingredients for the arepa in a large bowl and mix until well combined. Roll dough into 3–4 ounce balls and flatten to 1½-inch thickness. Thoroughly grease a large sauté pan or griddle, and cook arepas over medium-high heat until browned, about 2–3 minutes per side.

To make the avocado puree, combine all the ingredients in a food processer or blender and process until smooth, about 1 minute. Alternatively, mash the ingredients by hand with a potato masher. Set aside.

Mix the plantains, beans, cheese, and garlic in a medium bowl until well combined. Set aside.

To serve, split each arepa in half horizontally, leaving a hinge attached. Stuff with the browned pork belly, plantain mixture, jicama, hot sauce, and a dollop of avocado puree.

__Note:__ Masarepa flour, a dried, precooked ground corn flour used for arepas, can be found in most South American specialty markets. Different from masa harina, used for making tortillas, masarepa may also be labeled *masa al instante* or *harina precocida* by such brands as Goya, Juana, and Harina.

LOCKWOOD

17 EAST MONROE STREET, LOOP
(312) 917-3404
WWW.LOCKWOODRESTAURANT.COM
EXECUTIVE CHEF: GREG ELLIOTT

The historic Palmer House Hilton made its big-screen debut when actor Harrison Ford in *The Fugitive* loudly interrupts a presentation in the main ballroom to try and prove his innocence. While the story of the hotel itself spans 140 years, the younger Lockwood could easily stand on its own. With a strong reputation started by chef Philip Foss (see Mobile Food Trucks, page 112), successor Elliott has continued the farm-to-table tradition, stepping up efforts even more to build relationships with local chefs while bringing in a more rustic simplicity developed while working in California's wine country. Prior to that, Elliott learned fine dining at one sixtyblue and the now-shuttered institution Ambria.

Inside, Lockwood is covered head to toe in pristine white marble, from the walls and pillars and floors to the cocktail bar. Crystal chandeliers also help exude an elegance reminiscent of Audrey Hepburn in tiara, black gloves, and full *Breakfast at Tiffany's* garb.

"We see many guests from outside the hotel, so I'm trying to create a menu that's approachable, with something for everyone; simple and basic, but with a little element of surprise," Elliot says.

Dishes have ranged from local Heartland Meats smoked beef cheeks with sweet squash dumplings and blue cheese bread pudding to rack of Wisconsin-raised lamb with roasted Midwestern sunchokes and anchovy pesto. A baby beet salad also showcases the best of Midwestern bounty.

BABY BEET AND FARRO SALAD WITH AVOCADO, TARRAGON, AND GOAT'S MILK FETA

(Serves 4–6)

For the farro:

1 tablespoon extra-virgin olive oil
1 onion, diced
3 cups uncooked farro
Water or vegetable broth
Salt and pepper, to taste

For the beets:

1 pound trimmed baby beets
2 tablespoons extra-virgin olive oil
Salt and freshly ground black pepper

For the lemon vinaigrette and assembly:

½ cup fresh lemon juice
¼ cup sherry vinegar
1¼ cups plus 2 tablespoons extra-virgin olive oil,
   divided
Salt and freshly ground black pepper
2 shallots, sliced
3 tablespoons chopped fresh tarragon
Zest of 1 lemon
2 ripe avocados, in large dice
2 heads frisée, cleaned
1 cup crumbled goat's milk feta (preferably
   Redwood Hill Farms)
1 tablespoon honey

First, prepare the farro. Heat the oil in a sauté pan over medium heat and cook onions until lightly browned, about 5 minutes. Stir in farro and enough water or broth just to cover. Bring to a light simmer. Cook slowly, stirring occasionally and adding more water each time the liquid reduces. Continue cooking 30–35 minutes or until farro is tender. Season with salt and pepper to taste and refrigerate until chilled.

Preheat oven to 400°F. Toss beets with the olive oil, salt, and pepper to taste. Roast on a sheet pan for 40–45 minutes or until cooked through. Allow the beets to cool and remove the skin with a paring knife or paper towel. Quarter beets and reserve for salad.

To prepare the lemon vinaigrette, whisk together the lemon juice and vinegar. Slowly pour in 1¼ cups olive oil, whisking constantly. Season with salt and pepper to taste. In a large bowl, toss farro with half of the shallots and tarragon, the lemon vinaigrette, and the lemon zest. In another bowl, toss together the beets, avocados, and remaining shallots and tarragon.

To serve, toss the frisée with 1 tablespoon olive oil and salt and pepper to taste. Spoon the farro salad onto the bottom of a large platter and top with the beet mixture, frisée salad, and feta cheese. Drizzle honey and the remaining 1 tablespoon olive oil on and around the salad to finish.

Sola

3868 North Lincoln Avenue, North Center
(773) 327-3868
www.sola-restaurant.com
Chef-Owner: Carol Wallack

The chef's-jacket-with-shorts combo and long blond locks are a dead giveaway. Carol Wallack cooks by trade, but she's also a passionate surfer and lover of the sun. At Sola in the North Center neighborhood, Wallack brings her love of Hawaii (where she also owns a home) and California roots to both the menu and the ambience. Light wood and neutral coloring, soft lighting, and an overall casual approach with friendly servers and a fruity cocktail menu make Wallack's eatery feel like a sunny oasis, especially during the cold, often harsh winters.

In a modern-day fusion, Wallack's dishes draw from Hawaiian cuisine, such as poki (marinated fish) and Kahlúa-marinated pork, as well as from other Asian cuisines. While her hoisin-and-ginger-spiked short ribs have long lived as a best seller, Wallack excels at seafood, serving up mahimahi and other fresh fish with a gentle touch and carefully paired flavors.

"Everything is fresh, farm to table, and made here," Wallack says. "The Hawaiian culture is the one I love, and that's become an important part of my life, so I've tried to share it with others here."

Wallack's recipe for a simple yet elegant salad full of Asian flavors originally called for matsutake mushrooms—a rich, spicy mushroom with a robust stalk and a small round head. These delicacies can be pricey and hard to find. Oyster mushrooms, thanks to their strong umami flavor and meaty but delicate texture, make a good substitute. Ponzu, a Japanese citrus-based sauce, forms the base for a light vinaigrette.

CRISPY SHAVED MUSHROOM SALAD WITH PONZU VINAIGRETTE

(Serves 6)

For the ponzu sauce:

2½ tablespoons soy sauce
2 tablespoons freshly squeezed lemon juice
½ tablespoon rice vinegar
2½ tablespoons dashi stock, homemade or
    prepared from powder (traditional Japanese
    sea stock available in most markets)

For the vinaigrette:

1 small shallot, minced
1 tablespoon minced crystallized ginger
1 jalapeño pepper, seeded and minced
¼ cup rice vinegar
¾ cup canola or grapeseed oil

For the salad:

Vegetable or canola oil
6 matsutake mushrooms, shaved, or 12 oyster
    mushrooms, cut lengthwise into thin strips
6 cups packed arugula or baby arugula sprigs
6 small radishes, thinly sliced
1 Asian pear, cored and thinly sliced
1-ounce piece aged, sharp, nutty cheese
    (such as Upland Dairy's Pleasant Ridge Reserve
    or good-quality Parmigiana Reggiano)

To make the ponzu sauce, in a small bowl whisk together the soy sauce, lemon juice, vinegar, and dashi.

To make the vinaigrette, in a separate bowl whisk together the shallot, ginger, jalapeño, and vinegar. Add 2 tablespoons of the ponzu sauce, reserving extra for another use, if desired. Gradually drizzle in the oil, whisking constantly until emulsified. Refrigerate until serving.

To pan-fry the mushrooms, pour oil into a medium saucepan to a depth of about 1 inch. Heat the oil over medium-high heat until sizzling, or to 350–375°F. Add half of the mushrooms and fry until golden and crispy, 1–2 minutes. Use a slotted spoon to transfer mushrooms to paper towel to drain. Repeat with remaining mushrooms.

In a large bowl, toss the arugula, radish, and pear with 3 tablespoons of the vinaigrette. Add more vinaigrette as needed to lightly coat the salad without overdressing. Top the salad with the crispy mushrooms.

Using a vegetable peeler, cut long, wide shavings of the cheese over the salad for garnish.

Spiaggia

980 North Michigan Avenue, Mag Mile
(312) 280-2750
WWW.SPIAGGIARESTAURANT.COM
Owner: Levy Restaurants
Chef-Partner: Tony Mantuano
Executive Chef: Sarah Grueneberg

When there's talk about Chicago institutions Trotter's, Topolobampo, and Everest, Spiaggia will always make it into the conversation. Larry and Mark Levy, along with Tony Mantuano, one of the patriarchal chefs of the city's culinary scene, brought Italian cuisine to the fine-dining forefront in 1984, around the time Bayless did the same for Mexican, Joho for French, and Trotter for New American. A stomping ground for celebrities, dignitaries, and famous politicians including President Barack Obama, Spiaggia has also touched the hearts of all Chicago residents and visitors who dined there, with its sophistication in both cooking and service, its refined degustation menus, and its award-winning wine selection.

Post-recession, Mantuano has opened Café Spiaggia as a way to add more approachability and affordability to Spiaggia's legacy, one level below the main restaurant in a narrow space with a black-and-white tiled floor, lined with hand-painted murals of Italian scenes, like its fine-dining sibling upstairs, windows overlooking Chicago's Magnificent Mile. Mantuano has also become a bit of a TV celebrity, with appearances on popular chef shows, and he's teamed up with successful restaurateur Scott Harris for other ventures, including opening The Purple Pig (see page 120).

Under the guidance and mentorship of Mantuano, New Orleans–trained chef Sarah Grueneberg rose through the ranks from sous-chef in charge of purchasing to helming the kitchen. She continues Spiaggia's reputation for sophistication while also expanding upon the restaurant's long-held commitment to local and high-quality ingredients, and she adds a softer, feminine touch to the menu, starting with this popular focaccia bread using Taggiasca olives—small reddish-brown olives grown in the Liguria region on the northwest coast of Italy with a delicate, slightly fruity taste. If Taggiasca olives can't be found, substitute Gaeta or other semi-ripe olives and omit the salt in the stuffing mixture.

Stuffed Focaccia with Mozzarella, Taggiasca Olives, and Basil

(Serves 12–15)

For the dough:

2 packets (¼-ounce each) active dry yeast
Pinch of sugar
2 cups warm water (110°F)
6 tablespoons extra-virgin olive oil, divided
5 cups all-purpose flour
2 teaspoons sea salt
2 tablespoons corn meal

For the stuffing:

4 ounces fresh mozzarella cheese, thinly sliced
1 cup loosely packed basil leaves
½ cup (2 ounces) grated Parmigiana Reggiano
     cheese
1 cup pitted Taggiasca olives, divided
Sea salt and freshly ground black pepper, to taste

To make the dough, combine yeast, sugar, and water in a small bowl and let sit until bubbly, about 5 minutes. Stir in 2 tablespoons of the olive oil.

Add the flour and salt to the bowl of an electric stand mixer fitted with a dough hook. Add the yeast mixture and mix on low speed until the dough pulls away from the sides of the bowl, about 3–5 minutes.

Transfer the dough to a lightly oiled bowl. Turn over to coat lightly. Cover with a clean towel and let rise in a warm place 1 hour or until doubled in size.

Place dough on a countertop lightly dusted with flour. Knead dough until a smooth ball forms, about 5 minutes. Divide dough into 2 equal balls; cover with a clean towel or plastic wrap and let rest 15 minutes.

Preheat oven to 300°F. Brush a 12 x 18-inch baking sheet with 2 tablespoons of the olive oil and sprinkle with cornmeal. Press one ball of dough evenly into the baking pan to form the bottom crust.

Layer mozzarella cheese, basil, Parmigiana Reggiano cheese, and ¾ cup of the olives over crust. Season with salt and pepper to taste.

Roll out remaining ball of dough to the same size as the pan. Place over filled dough. Brush 2 tablespoons olive oil over dough. Garnish with the remaining olives by pushing them a half inch down into the top layer of dough. Cover with foil; bake for 30 minutes. Uncover; continue to bake 15 minutes, or until crust is golden brown and toothpick inserted in center comes out clean. Drizzle lightly with additional olive oil. Allow bread to cool in pan 20 minutes before slicing to serve.

WRIGLEY FIELD
HOME OF
CHICAGO CUBS
ComEd-PROVIDING
CUSTOMERS WITH RELIABLE
G

Pasta

Chicago has a rich Italian heritage, and that's reflected not only by Little Italy and the immigrants who wove the city's cultural fabric years ago, but also by the chefs who have devoted their work to this particular cuisine, and still others who have found inspiration in Italian ingredients and dishes. In many ways Italian food here, and nationwide, no longer is an "ethnic" food. It's become a way of eating, and a way of life.

Still, when we talk about pasta in relation to Chicago, other types of noodles mustn't go unnoticed. From the brothy, steaming bowls of ramen at Urban Belly and at Takashi on Sundays to the pho, pad thai, and udon noodle soup that abound everywhere in between, Chicago enjoys culinary influences from many Asian immigrants and neighborhood communities, including Japanese, Thai, and Korean, as well as Little Vietnam near Argyle Street and Chinatown further south.

PICCOLO SOGNO

464 North Halsted Street, River West
(312) 421-0077
www.piccolosognorestaurant.com
CHEF–CO-OWNER: TONY PRIOLO

Tony has a lot of friends. It started during his twelve-year tenure as executive chef of Coco Pazzo in River North, and now, at his own restaurant, he's a regular in the dining room, stretching tall and thin over the tables with a wide smile in tow. Piccolo Sogno, which translates literally to "little dream," is just that for Priolo and Naples-born business partner Ciro Longobardo.

Set in a little stand-alone building, a white marble bar at the front lures guests into the cozy dining room that, during the summer months, flows through open doors to the popular outdoor patio lined with garden beds where Priolo grows fresh herbs and vegetables for use in the kitchen. "We wanted to bring Italy to you," Priolo says of his Tuscany-focused eatery with dishes also blended with foods from other Italian regions.

Simple, seasonal, and with few ingredients but only the best ones—that's the motto of Italian cookery and what Priolo offers here. The menu changes frequently as a result, showcasing various local farms. Priolo even sent the restaurant's extra fennel, of which he says they use volumes, to a farm in Michigan that fed the vegetable to its pigs. Those pigs later became multiple nightly specials back at the restaurant. And, in the vein of a classic Italian restaurant, Piccolo Sogno's wine list spans 450 different bottles at affordable prices. For his four-cheese ravioli recipe, Priolo suggests looking for the best-quality cheeses possible because of the dish's simplicity, and when working with the dough, he recommends using a pasta roller, or a good rolling pin and strong arms.

PICCOLO SOGNO

Ravioli Quattro Formaggi (Four Cheese Ravioli)

(Serves 4, about 6 pieces each)

For the filling:

1 cup fresh ricotta cheese
2 tablespoons freshly grated Parmigiana Reggiano cheese
2 tablespoons Capriole Farms, locally sourced, or other good-quality goat cheese
2 tablespoons chopped Gorgonzola Dolcelatte cheese
1 teaspoon chopped Italian parsley
Sea salt and freshly ground black pepper, to taste

For the dough:

2¾ cups semolina flour
1¼ cups all-purpose flour
1 teaspoon sea salt
4 egg yolks, plus 1 yolk for egg wash
1 tablespoon olive oil
2 tablespoons water

For the Marsala glaze and sauce:

1 cup Marsala wine
½ cup chicken broth
1 teaspoon heavy cream
2 tablespoons unsalted butter, cut into cubes
Sea salt and freshly ground black pepper, to taste
1 tablespoon toasted pine nuts
Block of Parmigiana Reggiano cheese

For the filling, in a medium bowl combine the four cheeses, parsley, salt and pepper.

For dough place both flours and the salt in a food processor. Add 4 egg yolks and oil; pulse until dough forms a ball. (To prepare by hand, in a large bowl, make a well in the center of dry ingredients. Add 4 yolks and oil to the well; using a fork, beat the liquid until smooth and so that it picks up the dry ingredients. Keep mixing until dough forms a ball.)

Knead the dough by hand until slightly firm, similar in feel to your ear lobe. Add water, 1 teaspoon at a time, if dough becomes crumbly or too dry. Rest dough for 10 minutes.

Make the Marsala glaze. In a small saucepan over medium-high heat, cook wine until reduced to 2 or 3 tablespoons. Consistency should be thick and syrupy. Set aside.

Roll out the dough in one piece using a pasta machine or by hand until the dough is thin enough to see your hand through it. Brush dough with wash made of remaining egg yolk. Drop quarter-size dollops of the cheese filling about 1½ inches apart on one half of the dough. Fold opposite half of the dough over the filled side. Using an inverted shot glass, push down over a mound of filling, pressing air out. With a paring knife, cut around the glass to cut out the ravioli. Press the edges of each ravioli gently to seal. Cover with a damp cloth.

Next, prepare the sauce. In a medium saucepan over medium-high heat, reduce the chicken broth by half. Remove from heat, cool slightly, and add the cream and butter, stirring briskly with a wire whisk or fork until sauce is smooth. Season with salt and pepper.

Bring a large pot of water to a boil. Add the ravioli and cook until al dente, about 2 minutes. Drain and toss with sauce.

Divide ravioli among four plates or shallow bowls. Drizzle with Marsala glaze in a zigzag using a spoon or squirt bottle. Garnish with toasted pine nuts and shavings of Parmigiana Reggiano made using a vegetable peeler.

LITTLE ITALY

European awnings and sidewalk patios. Strolling young families and rustling leafy trees. Thick wooden doors and big storefront windows. The famous bright red sign for Al's #1 Italian Beef. Taylor Street, the heart of Little Italy, has kept its charm since Chicago's largest wave of Italian immigrants settled in this neighborhood in the early 1900s. These days, the transforming Near West Side neighborhood reflects a wider cross section of cultures and backgrounds, but its three main traits remain: tree-lined streets, friendly people, and, of course, delicious food.

When Al Capone finished his daily gangster activities, he likely feasted on a big bowl of pasta with a chunky red Bolognese sauce, or maybe a creamy risotto, on this side of the tracks. And although he started Chicago's bad rap as a mobster town, both Italian immigrants and Chicago residents continue to enjoy the legal favorites—baked clams with a garlicky breaded crust, popcorn calamari dipped in spicy tomato sauce, big chops of chicken, veal, pork chops, and steaks simply grilled with olive oil, thyme, and, of course, garlic.

Nowadays, old school serves alongside new school. Scott Harris, notable for starting the Mia Francesca empire that contemporized traditional Italian food for the masses in the early '90s with restaurants that were fun, informal, affordable, and yet trendy, has returned to his roots to help contemporize modern-day Little Italy. This has included moving and retooling the iconic Gennaro's, announcing plans for a kitschy meatball-only eatery, and opening up Davanti Enoteca, the answer for tapas-style Italian. In a reflection of his now-closed first small-plates concept, Francesca Fresco, this upscale rendition also presents a lineup of small plates, but with an added focus on high-quality, simple ingredients and thoughtfully paired wines, reminiscent of true regional Italian cuisine. Think: sautéed sardines, crispy pork belly, smooth ricotta, and honeycomb in a mason jar, risotto carbonara with a runny egg yolk.

Aside from Harris's creations, Taylor Street's eats also include sushi, Mexican, Indian, and a swath of other ethnic restaurants, thanks to a changing residential base. Set in the tri-Taylor area just west of the I-90/94 expressway and bordering the University of Illinois at Chicago's campus as well as the revamped University Village and West Loop neighborhoods, Taylor Street has seen an influx of young singles and new families in the last decade as gentrification, for better or worse, propelled the development of new condos and townhomes. Yet even with this new diversity, that roasted Italian beef sandwich, stuffed in a soft hoagie with hot peppers and dripping juices, still ranks number one among most.

BIN 36 / BIN WINE CAFÉ

BIN 36
339 NORTH DEARBORN STREET, RIVER NORTH
(312) 755-9463
WWW.BIN36.COM

BIN WINE CAFÉ
1559 NORTH MILWAUKEE AVENUE, WICKER PARK
(773) 486-2233
WWW.BINWINECAFE.COM
CO-OWNER–GENERAL MANAGER: DAN SACHS
EXECUTIVE CHEF: JOHN CAPUTO
CO-OWNER–WINE DIRECTOR: BRIAN DUNCAN

Wine lovers in Chicago think of Bin 36 as one of the first real wine bars in the city—a place where they can go to try different wines by the glass (up to fifty) and by the bottle, enjoy cheese pairings (again, fifty), and snack on sharable appetizers and fresh salads tossed with local farm ingredients. They can also talk with the sommelier, the chef, and each other in an open and friendly environment.

The concept certainly isn't new. But many say Bin 36 was ahead of its time when it opened just over a decade ago. This wine bar offered more than just the standard whites and reds, and more than just cheese and crackers. Chef John Caputo was part of the first wave of chefs to put out a full menu of seasonal, frequently changing dishes, years before the words "green" and "local" existed as we know them today. But as much as Bin 36 focuses on modern American dishes, Caputo has Italian roots, and that shows in his work. Often traveling back to Italy, Caputo works in good-quality olive oils, fine sea salts, naturally raised meats, and produce from nearby farms, and the restaurant's artisanal cheese program is one of the best. Of course, Caputo also has a penchant for making his own pasta in-house. "My philosophy of cooking has always been to buy the best ingredients and handle them as little as possible—in other words, not screw them up," he says.

Wine director Brian Duncan has reaped numerous accolades as one of the first, and certainly most awarded, sommeliers in the city. When most sommeliers plied their profession only at fine-dining and classic French restaurants, and only at tables ordering expensive bottles, Duncan came to Bin 36 and made wine approachable, affordable, and fun. Sporting tortoise shell glasses and always trendily dressed, Duncan is often spotted roaming about the dining room and bar, ready to give suggestions. He also leads wine education classes at the restaurant throughout the year.

The education continues on the menu, which since day one has offered Duncan's suggested wine pairings with every single dish, from a simple salad or appetizer to a decadent dessert. The wines are listed by their bin number in the restaurant, giving the restaurant both its name and its unique character. Bin 36 was also one of the first wine bar–restaurants to open up a retail section where patrons can buy the wine they loved at their last dinner, or choose the wine they want with the next one.

WILD MUSHROOM RAVIOLI WITH POACHED BAY SCALLOPS, ENGLISH PEA PUREE & MINT OIL

(Serves 6)

For the pasta dough:

14 ounces all-purpose flour
4 whole eggs

For the filling:

1 tablespoon olive oil
2 shallots, diced
3 cloves garlic, minced
4 ounces mixed-variety wild mushrooms, finely chopped
¼ cup white wine
4 sprigs fresh thyme, stems removed, chopped

¼ bunch parsley, chopped
¾ cup ricotta cheese
¼ cup mascarpone cheese
Salt and freshly ground black pepper, to taste

For the scallops:

2 tablespoons grapeseed oil
1 pound bay scallops
½ cup fish stock or broth
½ tablespoon cold butter, cut into cubes
Salt and freshly ground black pepper, to taste

For the pea puree:

4 cups water
½ teaspoon salt
2 cups shelled English peas
1 tablespoon butter, softened

For the mint oil:

5 fresh mint leaves
¼ cup grapeseed oil (or other neutral-tasting
   oil such as canola)

To prepare the pasta dough, place the flour in a large bowl and make a hole in the center. Break eggs into the hole and, using a fork, slowly mix them into the flour. When completely incorporated, transfer dough to a cutting board lightly dusted with flour. Knead dough by hand until smooth and slightly elastic. Wrap dough in plastic wrap and refrigerate for 30 minutes.

Meanwhile, prepare the filling. Heat the oil in a medium sauté pan over medium heat. Add shallots and garlic and cook over low heat until soft and translucent, about 2 minutes. Add mushrooms and cook slowly until mushrooms

have given up their juices. Add wine and cook until wine and mushroom juices have evaporated completely. Remove from heat, let stand until cool. Stir in the thyme, parsley, ricotta, and mascarpone. Season with salt and pepper.

Remove dough from refrigerator and let stand at room temperature for 10 minutes. Roll out dough using a pasta machine or by hand to a very thin sheet. Cut dough into two even-sized sheets. Place teaspoonfuls of the filling on one of the pasta sheets, spaced 2 inches apart. Cover with the second sheet and gently press down. Cut into squares by slicing between the fillings. Place ravioli on a sheet tray. Cover tightly and refrigerate for 10–20 minutes.

Meanwhile, prepare the mint oil. In a blender, puree the mint leaves and oil. Transfer to a bowl and set aside. Clean out blender.

For the pea puree, bring the water and salt to a boil in a small pot. Add the peas and cook until tender, about 1 minute. Drain peas and transfer to the blender; stir in butter, and puree until smooth. Set aside.

Bring a large pot of salted water to a boil and add the ravioli. Cook until just tender, about 4–5 minutes. Drain and set aside.

In a skillet over medium-high heat, add oil and cook the scallops until opaque and lightly browned on both sides but soft to the touch in the center, about 1 minute per side. Add the fish stock, then the butter, stirring until melted. Spoon liquid over the scallops while cooking until sauce is just thick enough to coat the back of a spoon. Season with salt and pepper.

To serve, spoon pea puree in a thin layer on each of six plates. Divide ravioli evenly among the plates. Top with scallops and a drizzling of the mint oil.

Convito Café

1515 Sheridan Road, Wilmette
(847) 251-3654
WWW.CONVITOCAFEANDMARKET.COM
Owner: Nancy Brussat
Executive Chef: Noe Sanchez

Restaurants average three years, at most, in lifespan. Successful places may last five, even ten years. Convito's legacy has spanned more than thirty, with three decades' worth of Italian comfort food, gourmet takeout, good service, and Nancy Brussat the brain behind it all.

"We opened as a small shop on Sheraton Road in 1980," Brussat says. "We served various prepared foods and deli goods, made some of our own sauces to go, and had a small, boutique wine department. Back then there were no gourmet prepared-food places like that. I'm not going to claim I knew what I was doing, but all of a sudden customers were flocking in to this little store, and I realized what we were doing was important."

Italian and ethnic delis are nothing new to Chicago, but most agree Convito was the first gourmet grocer, with its aged prosciutto, chef-made prepared dishes, homemade pasta and sauces, breads baked in-house, upscale pastries, a retail section with specialty finds, and one of the city's most extensive selections of handcrafted Italian wines, thanks to Brussat and her staff's years of research and travel. Violet Calderelli, an Italian-born chef who ran the kitchen when Convito first opened, came up with many of the dishes still popular today.

Two years after opening the first Convito location, Brussat relocated to a larger space in Wilmette's Plaza del Lago, where she expanded the shop to house a 28-seat full-service restaurant serving lunch and dinner.

In 1984 Brussat opened a second Convito store downtown in Chicago's Gold Coast neighborhood, including a 62-seat white-tablecloth restaurant and wine bar, but a kitchen fire in 1993 forced the closure of that spot. With ends come new beginnings, so while the Wilmette Convito continued on its path of success, Brussat opened Bêtise in a vacant space across the plaza. The new venture was Brussat's first foray into French cuisine, and the more upscale bistro became an institution for brunch, ladies who lunch, and a neighborhood favorite for dinner.

With the recession of 2008 hitting hard and Starbucks looking to expand from its tiny storefront to bigger space in the plaza, the coffee giant bought out Convito, at which point Brussat moved the store and restaurant into Bêtise's space, renaming it Convito Café & Market. Brussat also promoted to executive chef the young and vibrant Noe Sanchez, who had worked his way up through the kitchen ranks for thirteen years after starting as a humble dishwasher.

The rest is history, and the legendary Vi's tuna salad, rigatoni e noci (pasta with sharp Fontinella cheese, walnuts, scallions and creamy dressing), grab-and-go sauces, and a lasagna and cannelloni selection that would put Little Italy to shame, all live on. Here's an example for starters.

COUNTRY CANNELLONI
(Serves 6)

For the pasta and filling:

6 sheets lasagna pasta
¼ cup olive oil, divided
⅓ cup chopped mushrooms
⅓ cup chopped spinach
1¼ cups ricotta cheese
¾ cup shredded mozzarella cheese
¾ cup grated Parmesan cheese
1 cup cooked, diced chicken breast
1 egg, beaten
¼ teaspoon salt
¼ teaspoon freshly ground black pepper

For the sauce:

1 small onion, minced
1 28-ounce can imported tomatoes, drained and coarsely chopped
3 basil leaves
Salt and black pepper, to taste
½ cup mascarpone cheese

Cook lasagna according to package directions, or until al dente.* Drain and reserve.

Heat 2 tablespoons of the oil in a medium sauté pan over medium heat. Add mushrooms and cook until slightly golden and tender, about 4 minutes. Add spinach and cook until just wilted. Remove from heat and reserve.

To prepare the filling, mix together the ricotta, mozzarella, and Parmesan cheeses, chicken breast, egg, salt, and pepper in a large bowl until well combined.

In the skillet used for the mushrooms, heat the remaining 2 tablespoons oil over medium-high heat. Add the onions and sauté until golden brown and caramelized, about 10 minutes. Add the tomatoes, basil, salt, and pepper and continue to cook until sauce begins to thicken, about 15 minutes. Strain sauce and fold in the mascarpone cheese.

Preheat oven to 350°F. Butter a 9 x 13-inch baking dish. Coat the bottom of the dish with a thin layer of the sauce. Cut lasagna sheets in half to make 4-inch squares. Divide the filling into twelve portions. To form the cannelloni, spread filling evenly along one edge of each square. Carefully roll up pasta and place in baking dish, seam side down. Top the cannelloni with the remaining sauce and bake for 30 minutes, or until bubbling.

Note: Fresh pasta can be purchased in many stores like Convito. Usually cannelloni squares, which are cut from fresh strips of lasagna, need to be ordered. Or make your own fresh pasta, rolling it out in wide strips with a pasta machine and cutting the strips into squares.

Mana Food Bar

1742 West Division Street, Wicker Park
(773) 342-1742
www.manafoodbar.com
Chef-Owner: Jill Barron

"The essence, or a life force, of nature. The essence of magic." That's the meaning behind the indigenous Pacific Islander word *mana*, according to Jill Barron. A Chicago native who spent time in California with chef Mary Sue Milliken of Border Grill, Barron picked up the free-spirited nature of the sunny state that also meant a penchant for eating less meat. Mana Food Bar represents one of the few vegetarian-friendly restaurants in meat-centric Chicago, but Barron is quick to point out she doesn't take the "fake" meat route of tempeh in the form of "unappealing" pretend turkey roasts and pork chops. Instead she uses the "magic" of her creative cooking, built up from years of opening renowned restaurants in Chicago, combined with a healthier approach to eating and dining.

"I felt that there was a need for this meatless way of eating because, for one thing, that's how I wanted to eat, and I wasn't finding anything geared toward that in Chicago," Barron says. "I wanted to create a global menu with a focus on different ethnic cuisines that were meatless and also delicious."

At the time, Chicago was certainly ready for the change. Since opening, Barron packs her place to the gills, with vegetarians and vegans, but also with meat lovers looking for a change of pace with a meatless meal. Her sesame noodles are simple and easy, but elevated in flavor by gentle ginger and spicy Sriracha.

Sesame Noodles with Peanut Dressing
(Serves 4)

For the peanut dressing:

2 tablespoons sesame seed paste
1 teaspoon peanut butter
1 tablespoon sugar
1 tablespoon chopped ginger
1 tablespoon chopped garlic
1 tablespoon Sriracha or other hot sauce
1 tablespoon sesame oil
1½ tablespoons soy sauce
1 teaspoon rice vinegar
Salt, to taste

For the sesame noodles and garnish:

1 8-ounce bag Chinese yellow noodles,
    cooked and chilled

1 carrot, peeled and shredded
12 pea pods, shredded
1 cup daikon sprouts
½ cup chopped roasted peanuts

In a food processor or blender, place the sesame paste, peanut butter, sugar, ginger, garlic, and Sriracha, and pulse until coarsely blended. Slowly pour in the oil and continue to pulse. Pour in the soy sauce and vinegar and pulse until smooth and creamy.

In a large bowl, place the noodles, carrot, and pea pods. Pour in dressing and toss until well combined. Garnish with the sprouts and chopped peanuts.

THE FLORENTINE

151 WEST ADAMS STREET, THE LOOP
(312) 660-8866
WWW.JWMARRIOTTCHICAGO.COM
EXECUTIVE CHEF: TODD STEIN
MANAGING COMPANY: BLT RESTAURANT GROUP

Todd Stein made a name for himself first at the legendary MK and later as executive chef at the Wit Hotel's Cibo Matto, once declared one of the best new restaurants in the country. When he moved to The Florentine, he brought the duck egg carbonara that made thousands of Chicago diners and visitors salivate over homemade noodles topped with smoky pancetta and a silky yolk that runneth all over.

At The Florentine, a New York City–based BLT Restaurant Group concept, Stein also brings his lifelong love of Italian cuisine, deepened by traveling and cooking in that food- and wine-focused country.

"I cook as though I'm an Italian chef in Chicago," Stein says. That means a focus on simple but refined cooking and the use of just a few high-quality ingredients in the form of seasonal finds from Illinois, Indiana, Michigan, and Ohio.

And in a setting that's part dining room, part private space, and part lively bar, all housed within the glitzy JW Marriott in the heart of the Loop's financial district, The Florentine attracts just as diverse a group of eaters, from nearby Mercantile Exchange traders and high-powered executives at lunch to foodie brunchgoers and couples seeking a glamorous night out for dinner.

That diversity in space also translates to the menu, from pizzas crisped in a wood-fired oven to other tasty small plates like a grilled octopus appetizer on a bed of springy frisée with hearty white beans, big parsley leaves, and a saffron aioli, as well as grown-up entrees like red-wine-braised short ribs, charred rare tuna, and homemade pastas including, of course, the carbonara. In this recipe, substitute good-quality, fresh-from-the-farm hen's eggs if duck eggs are not available.

DUCK EGG CARBONARA
(serves 2)

12 ounces bucatini pasta*
1 tablespoon extra-virgin olive oil
5 ounces pancetta, cut into ¼-inch dice
½ cup freshly grated pecorino Romano
   cheese, divided

2 teaspoons cracked black pepper, divided
¼ cup coarsely chopped parsley
2 duck egg yolks

In a large pot of boiling salted water, cook the pasta until al dente. Drain, reserving 3 tablespoons of the cooking water.

Meanwhile, heat the oil in a large skillet. Add the pancetta and cook over moderate heat until most of the fat has been rendered, about 7 minutes. Add the hot pasta to the skillet and stir to coat, 1 minute. Remove from the heat. Stir in the reserved pasta cooking water, ¼ cup of the grated cheese, and 1 teaspoon of the pepper.

Divide hot pasta evenly between two bowls and sprinkle with the remaining pepper and cheese and the parsley. Place 1 duck egg yolk on top of each pasta dish and serve immediately.

Note: Bucatini is a spaghetti-like pasta, but thicker and with hollow strands. Commonly eaten in Rome, the tubular pasta can be purchased at most grocery stores.

UNCOMMON GROUND

1214 WEST GRACE STREET, LAKEVIEW
(773) 929-3680
WWW.UNCOMMONGROUND.COM

1401 WEST DEVON AVENUE, EDGEWATER
(773) 465-9801
WWW.UNCOMMONGROUND.COM

OWNERS: HELEN AND MICHAEL CAMERON
EXECUTIVE CHEF: JUSTIN MARTIN

At the height of the Slow Food and "locavore" movement in Chicago, there was Uncommon Ground. When husband-wife owners Helen and Michael Cameron opened the second outpost further north in Edgewater, they dug five feet below ground to renovate the space with recycled and reclaimed materials. They also hired an architect with LEED (Leadership in Energy and Environmental Design) accreditation, meaning certified in "green," sustainable building design, to help create the certified-organic rooftop garden for herbs, flowers, and vegetables, many of them heirloom, to supplement the restaurant's season-driven menu using organics as well as produce and meats grown and raised on farms in Illinois and the Midwest. The restaurant has also used the green space as an educational tool for children and other city residents invested in urban agriculture initiatives. This includes installing two beehives to provide pollination for the plants as well as to help protect a species nearing endangerment.

At the original location, an expansive curved wooden bar hand-carved out of reclaimed wood by the restoration artist next door serves as the focal point of the room, outfitted in more light-colored woods, neutrals, and multicolored paintings and other artwork by local artists. The local support extends to the bar program as well, with large jugs of organic Rain vodka infused with seasonal and rare fruits, like moonglow pears grown in Chicago orchards developed by the Chicago Rarities Orchard project, a nonprofit organization committed to reclaiming space for preserving thousands of tree fruit varieties not grown commercially. For each cocktail ordered with the vodka, Uncommon Ground commits to planting a tree, and the restaurant has worked with the Rain distillery to order the spirit in the bulk jars as a way to

cut down on excess packaging.

It's this attention to detail that has helped Uncommon Ground earn numerous accolades for its sustainability initiatives. Chef Justin Martin carries that focus on detail to the menu, a fusion of American comfort food dishes with ethnic and Midwestern influences. For this pasta recipe, Martin uses Illinois spinach and onions, mushrooms from River Valley Ranch, and Gorgonzola from an artisan cheesemaker in Wisconsin, along with bacon sourced from a small pork-producing family farm. For a vegetarian option, simply omit the bacon. Either way, focusing on sourcing the best-quality ingredients for this simple pasta will work.

Homemade Ricotta Cavatelli with Mushrooms, Spinach, Caramelized Onion, Gorgonzola Cream, and Crispy Bacon

(Serves 4)

For the cavatelli:

8½ ounces all-purpose flour
3 ounces durum flour
2 teaspoons salt
1 teaspoon freshly ground black pepper
1 farm egg
8 ounces ricotta cheese

For the Gorgonzola cream:

4 ounces heavy whipping cream
6 ounces cream cheese
8 ounces crumbled Gorgonzola cheese
Salt and freshly ground black pepper, to taste

For the garnish

12 ounces sliced bacon
1 pound yellow onions, sliced ¼ inch thick
2 tablespoons extra-virgin olive oil, divided
8 ounces mushrooms, any variety,
    sliced ¼ inch thick
8 ounces fresh spinach leaves
4 tablespoons butter
Salt and pepper, to taste

For the cavatelli, mix the dry ingredients in a large bowl. In a separate bowl, whisk the egg and ricotta. Make a well in the dry ingredients and add the wet ingredients. Gently combine by hand until a uniform ball of dough is formed. Let rest 30 minutes.

On a lightly floured surface, roll out dough to ¼-inch thickness and cut into 1-inch strips. Run strips through a pasta machine or electric stand mixer fitted with a cavatelli (shell-shaped) maker attachment. Place pasta on a cookie sheet lined with wax paper and refrigerate.

For the Gorgonzola cream, combine heavy cream and cream cheese in a small, heavy-bottomed saucepan. Cook over low heat until cream cheese is melted, stirring frequently. Gradually add Gorgonzola a little at a time until melted. Season to taste with salt and pepper. Set aside and keep warm.

Heat oven to 350°F. Place bacon in a 15 x 10-inch jelly roll pan in a single layer. Bake until crispy, about 8–10 minutes. Crumble and reserve.

Sauté onions in 1 tablespoon of the oil in a large, heavy-bottomed sauté pan over medium-high heat until caramelized, about 10 minutes. Set aside and keep warm. In same pan, sauté mushrooms in remaining 1 tablespoon oil over medium-high heat until mushrooms release their liquid and liquid is absorbed. Reserve with the caramelized onions.

Bring 1 gallon water to a boil; add cavatelli. Stir once a minute for about 4 minutes until cavatelli is al dente. Drain, reserving ¼ cup of the cooking liquid.

In a sauté pan over medium heat, combine reserved pasta water, onions, mushrooms, spinach, and butter. Heat gently until the spinach wilts and butter is melted. Add cavatelli; toss gently. Season to taste with salt and pepper. Place ¼ cup of the warm Gorgonzola cream in each of four shallow bowls. Spoon cavatelli over Gorgonzola cream; top with bacon. Serve with remaining Gorgonzola cream.

FISH

It's 5 a.m. and the sun's nowhere in sight. Cutting through the cold darkness, trucks loaded with the day's freshest catch make their way through the quiet streets of the meatpacking district, former home to the stockyards infamously described in Upton Sinclair's *The Jungle*. A brave resident here or there shuffles in and out of the wholesaler warehouses, carrying mesh bags full of shrimp and lobsters packed on ice. The rest of the loot will go off to the restaurants come daybreak.

Historically, Chicago is a meat town. But thanks to O'Hare International Airport's status as one of the largest and busiest airports in the United States, Chicago has easy access to fish flown in daily from all parts of the world.

Cold-water oysters on the half shell, jumbo shrimp cocktail, whole lobsters with drawn butter, Parmesan-crusted baked clams. Seafood has a long history in Chicago, starting at the steakhouses in the '20s and '30s, and later at Italian restaurants looking to incorporate shellfish into big bowls of homemade pasta.

Now fresh fish is everywhere in Chicago, from sushi powerhouses like Mirai and Japonaise to the big-ticket hotels like the Affinia (C-House) and the Trump Tower where guests and locals alike expect only the finest quality. At Sixteen, chef Frank Brunacci once devoted a whole month to lobster, creating a prix fixe menu revolving around the delicacy. And the successful Boka Restaurant Group went all-seafood in the launch of its fourth concept, GT Fish & Oyster, named after chef Giuseppe Tentori, who offers his take on the classic New England clam chowder.

C-House

166 East Superior Street, Streeterville
(312) 523-0923
WWW.C-HOUSERESTAURANT.COM
Chef-Proprietor: Marcus Samuelsson
Executive Chef: Nicole Pederson

The brainchild of Ethiopian-born, New York–based Marcus Samuelsson, C-House breathed new life into the Affinia Hotel, once a sleepy boutique on the outskirts of Northwestern University's downtown law school and medical campus.

Samuelsson also brought a sense of stardom as a celebrity chef who took home the win on Bravo! TV's first season of *Top Chef: Masters.* In the early days, Samuelsson focused his menu on simple prime chops paired with refined seafood dishes. Now, with chef Nicole Pederson taking the helm so Samuelsson could return to his first restaurants, the menu showcases even more the best of the Midwest as well as a continued emphasis on pure flavors, simplicity, and seasonality. Pederson, who quickly won multiple awards after taking over the kitchen, in this way clearly remains true to her strong Midwestern roots as a Minnesota native. In fact, Samuelsson once referred to Pederson as "akin to a young Alice Waters with a passion for pure, simple food and a true understanding of the beauty in flavor combinations."

At the same time, Pederson shares a mastery of seafood cookery with her mentor, as well as a penchant for classic culinary technique due to time spent in France. Pederson continued to hone her skills at the famed Gramercy Tavern in New York City and, back at home, at Lula Café. One of her highest honors, she says, was assisting Samuelsson at the White House during his guest chef appearance for the Obama administration's first state dinner, preparing a meal for Prime Minister Singh of India and 400 guests. She has also assisted Samuelsson during dinners at the James Beard Foundation's prestigious Beard House in New York City. Her recipe for a smoked trout terrine demonstrates her love of seafood, French technique, and Midwestern ingredients, such as beets. Here she uses the savory-sweet root vegetable in a chrain, a traditional Eastern European horseradish root sauce stained red from beet juice and often eaten during Jewish holidays.

Smoked Trout and Lentil Terrine with Watercress and Creamy Caraway Salad and Pumpernickel Toast
(Serves 6)

For the terrine:

1 garlic clove, minced
2 tablespoons chopped shallots
½ teaspoon freshly grated horseradish root
1 tablespoon extra-virgin olive oil, plus more
   if needed

3 tablespoons chopped parsley
2 tablespoons chopped chives
¼ teaspoon salt
4 smoked trout fillets

For the vegetable stock and aspic:

2 cups water
1 clove crushed garlic
½ shallot, sliced
3 1-inch chunks fresh horseradish root
¼ teaspoon salt
3 sheets gelatin
2 cups soft-cooked French green lentils

For the watercress salad and toast:

1 teaspoon caraway seed, toasted and
   slightly crushed
½ cup sherry vinegar
3 tablespoons chopped shallot
3 egg yolks
1½ cups extra-virgin olive oil
¼ teaspoon each salt and freshly ground
   black pepper, or to taste
1 bunch fresh watercress, stems removed
3 slices pumpernickel bread, toasted and
   cut in halves

Cook the minced garlic, chopped shallots, and grated horseradish in 1 tablespoon olive oil over medium heat until soft and translucent. Transfer the mixture, including the oil, to a blender or food processor. Add the parsley, chives, salt, and skinned trout fillets. Pulse until smooth and creamy, about 3 minutes. Add more oil if mixture is too dry.

For the vegetable stock, heat the water, crushed garlic, shallot slices, and horseradish root in a small saucepan over medium heat. Reduce liquid to about 1¼ cups, season with salt, and strain into another small pot or bowl.

To prepare the aspic, bloom the gelatin in enough cool water to cover for 5 minutes or until soft. Squeeze out any extra liquid and add to the warm vegetable stock to dissolve.

Next, build the terrine. In a 9 x 5-inch loaf pan lined with plastic wrap, press one-third of the lentils along the bottom of the pan. Top with one-third of the aspic, then one-third of the trout, pressing layers gently into the pan to form a compact loaf. Repeat the layering process in the same order, twice, ending with the trout. Wrap tightly and refrigerate for at least 30 minutes to 1 hour.

For the watercress salad, first make the creamy caraway dressing. Whisk together the caraway, vinegar, shallot, and yolks in a small bowl. Slowly pour in the olive oil, whisking constantly, until dressing is creamy but not too thick. Season with salt and pepper. Alternatively, combine all the ingredients in a blender or food processor on low speed and slowly pour in the oil. In a separate bowl, gently toss the watercress with 2–3 tablespoons of the dressing, adding more if necessary. Any leftover dressing may be kept in the refrigerator for up to 24 hours.

To serve, flip the terrine upside down and lift off the pan and plastic wrap. Cut terrine into 1½-inch-thick slices and place one slice off-center on each of six plates and top evenly with the watercress-caraway salad. Add a half slice of pumpernickel toast to each plate.

Sixteen

401 North Wabash Avenue, River North
(312) 588-8030
WWW.TRUMPCHICAGOHOTEL.COM
EXECUTIVE CHEF: THOMAS LENTS
FORMER EXECUTIVE CHEF: FRANK BRUNACCI

Sixteen—the floor of the restaurant, but also a symbol of grace, magic, and some Midwestern hospitality without the snobbery or ego one would think naturally accompanies a big-city, skyscraping glass tower under the Donald Trump name.

The Michelin-starred magnificence continues in the dining room, with wintery-white leather seats, full-length mirrors, and a massive crystal chandelier. Then there are the dramatic floor-to-ceiling windows overlooking the Trump's terrace bar and, beyond, the historic buildings lining the Chicago River. At night it's like a fairy tale, with the almost century-old Wrigley Building illuminated by colorful lights.

Dishes have a fine-dining, super-creative, almost whimsical quality on what's said to be the largest plate budget in the city. Former Chef Frank Brunacci planted those roots as the first chef to head up the restaurant. Case in point: His idea of an amuse-bouche was a custom-made, rectangular plate with an imprint for a single crouton.

Though Brunacci's since left, Trump daughter Ivanka has been known, then and now, to hang in the kitchen, snacking on Brunacci's delicate dishes. A Melbourne native, Brunacci was a seafood, particularly lobster, master. His legacy remains.

LOBSTER ROLLS
(Makes 4 sandwiches)

1 cup mayonnaise
2 stalks celery, leaves removed, sliced
    into ½-inch pieces
1 bunch green onions, thinly sliced
Juice of 1 lemon
1 tablespoon finely chopped flat-leaf parsley
2 tablespoons thinly sliced basil
1 teaspoon salt
½ teaspoon freshly ground black pepper
4 cups chopped lobster meat
4 New England–style brioche buns, split vertically
2 tablespoons unsalted butter, softened
2 tablespoons hot, Dijon mustard
1 tablespoon honey
1 cup shredded romaine lettuce (optional)
Thinly sliced cornichons and jalapeños (optional)

Combine the mayonnaise, celery, onions, lemon juice, parsley, basil, salt and pepper in a large bowl. Fold in lobster meat and mix well.

Spread the outsides of each bun evenly with butter. Toast buns in a dry skillet or oven until golden brown, about 1–2 minutes per side.

Mix together the mustard and honey. Spread mixture evenly along the insides of the buns. Fill with shredded lettuce, if desired, then the lobster salad. Top with cornichons and jalapeños, if desired.

Sepia

123 North Jefferson Street, West Loop
(312) 441-1920
WWW.SEPIACHICAGO.COM
Owner: Emmanuel Nony
Executive Chef: Andrew Zimmerman

The muted, warm tones of a sepia photograph created by flash cameras in the 1800s also color Sepia the restaurant like a vintage snapshot from a pre-Prohibition cocktail bar. In fact, the first thing one sees on walking in is the lounge area, situated along the front windows overlooking Clinton Street, with low-slung booths, a mahogany bar, retro glassware, and plenty of rye- and gin-based cocktails dreamed up by various mixologists that have come and gone.

Beyond the bartenders sits the more intimate dining area, draped in more soft browns, beiges, and warmed-up grays with a few oversized cylindrical chandeliers for a pop of brightness and spirit. In the kitchen the sense of mystery and old-fashioned drama continues with chef Andrew Zimmerman's creative masterpieces served prettily like paintings on a canvas of plain white ceramic alongside a wine list with just as much refinement, grace, and balance.

"A lot of the dishes we do start off at least inspired by classic, rustic cooking, and then we take a contemporary approach to it," he says. "We're also committed to trying to use as much seasonal, local, and organic product as we can."

That's evident in one springtime menu favorite—a simple English pea and mascarpone ravioli with thyme butter, pea shoots, pickled shallots, and mint. Another successful dish took shape as a poached duck egg served over a ragout of morel mushrooms and a confit of duck gizzards. And his latest experiment, a plump bone-marrow-and-egg-based dumpling, breaded and shaped around liquefied fois gras in an oxtail consommé for a pop-in-your-mouth factor, proved particularly popular. In this bass recipe, the simple and sweet corn chowder reflects the flavors of the Midwest.

WILD STRIPED BASS WITH SWEET CORN CHOWDER AND LITTLENECK CLAMS
(Serves 4)

4 ears sweet corn, kernels removed
2 leeks, white part only, diced
3 stalks celery heart, chopped
2 medium carrots, peeled and diced
1 medium onion, diced
4 sprigs fresh thyme
1 bay leaf
¼ cup plus 1 tablespoon extra-virgin
   olive oil, divided
1½ pounds young potatoes (fingerling,
   German butterball), chopped
16 pearl onions, peeled
2 cups heavy cream, reduced to 1 cup
12 littleneck clams, scrubbed
¼ cup chopped flat-leaf parsley
Salt and freshly ground black pepper
4 6-ounce fillets wild-caught striped bass, skin on

Reserve ¼ cup of the corn kernels for garnish. In a large stockpot, combine half of the leeks, celery, carrots, and diced onion, plus ½ cup corn kernels, 2 sprigs thyme, and the bay leaf. Pour in enough cold water to cover by about 2 inches and bring to a boil. Reduce heat and simmer 40 minutes.

Strain the corn broth, discarding the solids. Wash out the stockpot and heat 1 tablespoon oil over medium heat. Add the remaining leeks, celery, carrots, and diced onion, and the remaining corn kernels. Season with a pinch of salt and cook until onions are soft and translucent, about 2–3 minutes.

Add the corn broth, remaining 2 sprigs thyme, potatoes, pearl onions, and cream. Simmer chowder until potatoes are tender, about 20 minutes. Add the clams and continue to cook until shells just begin to open. Add the parsley and season with salt and pepper as needed.

Heat the remaining ¼ cup oil in large sauté pan over medium-high heat. Season the bass with salt and pepper and cook, skin side down, about 4–5 minutes, or until skin is crispy and golden. Flip fillets and continue to cook until opaque and just cooked through, another 2–3 minutes.

To plate the chowder, scoop the chowder vegetables and clams evenly into four shallow bowls. Pour in broth and top each bowl with a bass fillet, skin side up. Garnish with remaining ¼ cup corn kernels.

Perennial Virant

1800 North Lincoln Avenue, Lincoln Park
(312) 981-7070
www.perennialchicago.com
Owners: Kevin Boehm and Rob Katz
Executive Chef: Paul Virant

Whimsical. Playful. Seasonal, yet rustic and approachable. These are the attributes that best described not only the restaurant's original chef, Ryan Poli, but also this current culinary theater. Part of the rapidly growing Boka Restaurant Group enterprise, it has undergone a name, décor, and chef change to become Perennial Virant, directed by locavore leader Paul Virant of Vie (page 2). Regardless of the changes, the emphasis on Green City Market and other Midwestern foods continues.

Dark wood throughout in floor, ceiling beams and furniture, offset by paintings and photos of farm scenes and a plant-friendly, sidewalk patio create an airy, open-barn feel. That ambience is further intensified by floor-to-ceiling windows overlooking the grassy, tree-lined Lincoln Park, where Green City Market (see page 10) sets up during the spring and summer where most, if not all, of the menu's fresh foods are sourced. At the front, a small but energetic bar sends out imaginative cocktails put together by master mixologists and a slew of rotating guest creators.

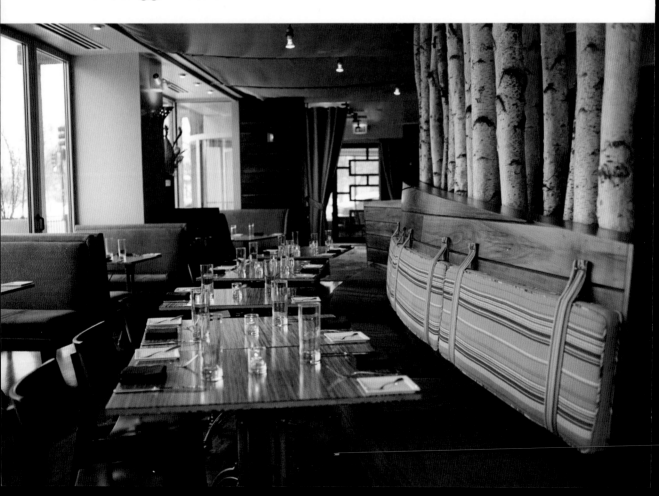

Even after Poli's departure, his mark on the menu remains. Here, for his deconstructed fish taco recipe, Poli attempts to re-create the traditional flavors of a taco, even though the dish may not resemble one at first glance. Corn nut essence replaces tortillas. And a smooth avocado puree represents a scoop of guacamole. Substitute any fresh, sashimi-grade fish if hiramasa is unavailable or hard to find.

Deconstructed Fish Tacos with Avocado Puree and Corn Nut Mousse
(Serves 4)

For the corn nut mousse:

½ cup heavy whipping cream
¼ cup milk
¾ cup corn nuts

For the mango relish:

2 tablespoons finely diced mango
2 tablespoons finely chopped pineapple
2 tablespoons finely chopped papaya
2 tablespoons finely chopped cilantro
2 tablespoons freshly squeezed lime juice
2 tablespoons finely chopped tomato
½ teaspoon minced serrano chile
Salt, to taste

For the avocado puree:

2 ripe avocados, peeled and pitted
Freshly squeezed lime juice and salt to taste

For the lemon vinaigrette and fish:

1 tablespoon freshly squeezed lemon juice
2 tablespoons grapeseed oil
Salt to taste
20 sashimi slices of hiramasa (yellowtail kingfish)
Sea salt, to taste
Zest of one lime

First, prepare the corn nut mousse. Bring cream and milk just to a boil and pour over corn nuts in a bowl. Cover and refrigerate at least 8 hours.

Next, prepare the mango relish. Combine all the ingredients in a bowl, season with salt. Refrigerate for 2–4 hours, up to overnight.

Puree avocados in a blender or food processor until smooth. Season with lime juice and salt. Cover with plastic wrap and refrigerate.

Strain the cream mixture, discarding corn nuts. In an electric stand mixer fitted with a whisk attachment, or using a handheld electric mixer, whip the cream mixture until frothy. Set aside.

Make the vinaigrette by whisking together the lemon juice and oil. Season with salt. Gently toss the fish with the vinaigrette to coat lightly.

To serve, on each of four plates arrange mango relish in a straight line down the center. Place 3 to 5 small dollops of the avocado alongside the mango relish. Place small dollops of the corn nut mousse between the avocado mounds. Lay 5 pieces of fish per plate side by side over the line of mango relish. Sprinkle fish with a little sea salt and lime zest and serve immediately.

Boka

1729 North Halsted Street, Lincoln Park
(312) 337-6070
www.bokachicago.com
Owners: Kevin Boehm and Rob Katz
Executive Chef: Giuseppe Tentori

Giuseppe Tentori exploded on the scene when he took over the Boka kitchen years ago, declared Best New Chef that year by various outlets. Since then, he's remained committed to serving up seasonal finds, built upon his strong relationships with Midwestern farms.

When it comes to the menu, the Italian-accented chef says, "We keep it not just American contemporary, but most of our food is very light. Not too much butter, cream, or dairy. More olive oil and broth."

A garden-lined stone walkway leads up to the main doorways with the bar and lounge area to the left and the main dining space to the right, designed by renowned New York City–based architect and designer Warren Ashworth, whom the Boehm-Katz powerhouse also recruited to create the similarly whimsical, mystical Perennial space. Light neutrals, soft lighting, fabric-draped ceilings, and a slightly minimalist approach in the dining room create the perfect canvas for Tentori's artfully composed dishes abstractly painted on stark white china plates in squares, rectangles, and triangles.

After a short hiatus, Giuseppe's famed tasting menus are back with optional pairings from his boutique list. At the bar, mixologist Benjamin Schiller works like an alchemist, whipping up his own bitters, essential oils, herbal reductions, and other potions for both creative and classic cocktails.

The Boka group's latest endeavor, GT Fish & Oyster, using Tentori's initials, opens up as a much more casual space. Craft beers on tap and a slew of fresh oysters and fish crudo get served at the bar, an 18-foot-long focal point made out of repurposed surfboard. Classic dishes like lobster roll, fish and chips, and calamari, plus more creative ones like paella-stuffed squid with chorizo, shrimp, and saffron grace the seafood-focused menu. Here Tentori

offers the clam chowder he took months to perfect, first serving the soup alongside the New American dishes that make up the menu at Boka. Tentori uses diamondback clams from New Zealand for their meaty texture and umami taste, dropping them into the simmering stock just before serving to prevent rubberiness from overcooking. For this recipe, any whole clams may be used.

GT's Clam Chowder

(Serves 4, each portion 8 ounces)

3 ounces diced bacon
7 ounces chopped onion
4 ounces chopped celery
1 ounce chopped garlic
6 ounces white wine, divided
10 ounces clam juice
12 ounces heavy cream
5 sprigs fresh thyme
1 bay leaf
1 pound diced Yukon Gold potatoes
2 tablespoons cornstarch
2 tablespoons cold water
2 pounds whole clams
1 tablespoon butter
1 tablespoon extra-virgin olive oil
1 tablespoon chopped shallot
Salt and freshly ground black pepper, to taste
Chopped fresh chives, for garnish
Dash Tabasco sauce or other hot pepper sauce

Cook bacon in a large saucepan over medium heat 5 minutes. Add onion, celery, and garlic and cook 1 minute. Add 3 ounces wine; reduce until the alcohol has cooked off, about 2 minutes. Add clam juice, heavy cream, thyme sprigs, and bay leaf; bring slowly to a simmer.

Add potatoes and cook at a low simmer over medium-low heat for 15 minutes. Do not boil or soup will break. In a small bowl, mix cornstarch and water until smooth, and stir mixture into

soup. Simmer until thickened to a chowder consistency. Discard thyme sprigs and bay leaf and set pan aside.

Wash clams thoroughly, making sure to rid them of any residual sand. Melt butter with olive oil in a large sauté pan over medium heat. Add shallot and cook 1 minute. Add remaining 3 ounces wine and bring to a simmer. Add clams and cook for about 5 minutes, or until shells open. Gently stir clam mixture into the chowder. Season chowder with salt and pepper to taste. Ladle into four bowls. Garnish with chives and Tabasco sauce and serve with a crusty baguette.

THE SOUTHERN

1840 WEST NORTH AVENUE, WICKER PARK
(773) 342-1840
WWW.THESOUTHERNCHICAGO.COM
CO-OWNER–EXECUTIVE CHEF: CARY TAYLOR
CO-OWNER: JIM LASKY

It took a few tries until they got it right. Before it was The Southern, this Miami-meets-Wicker Park indoor-outdoor restaurant and lounge was Chaise Lounge with a more contemporary American menu. Before that, another chef led the kitchen. Finally, current chef Cary Taylor has been able to spread his Southern wings, cooking the comfort food he grew up with in Georgia, but with a twist scaled up enough to match the trend-setting, well-heeled crowds.

The Miami reference stems from the outdoor patio lined with garden walls, the soft night lighting, chic umbrella-covered tables, and doors to the inside that remain open during warmer months. Inside, soft white leather booths add to this look, as well as to the function of the space—long enough to seat eight, ten, or more, they're perfect for Taylor's Sunday fried chicken deals accommodating bigger groups who order ahead for the big feast. Perhaps it's the crispy, crackly crunch of the chicken, the buttery biscuits, or the spicy cocktails that have caused The Southern to outshine its former concept. Or maybe it's the youthful, free-spirited personality that Taylor carries into the dining room when doing rounds. Outside the restaurant's walls, Taylor takes his meals on wheels with The Southern's Mac & Cheese truck, attracting swarms of hungry lunchers with every Twitter-based "tweet" like bees to honey.

Above all, Taylor's a trained classic chef, working under the finest chefs in the city as a fine-dining protégé. Here his crab cakes seem simple and Southern to boot. But with a spiced-up kick, Taylor demonstrates his diversity in both resume and capability.

SPICY CRAB CAKES AND PETITE SALADE WITH MUSTARD VINAIGRETTE
(Serves 8)

For the salad:

¼ cup red wine vinegar
2 teaspoons hot mustard
1 cup extra-virgin olive oil
Kosher or sea salt and freshly ground
    black pepper, to taste
8 cups arugula or baby spinach leaves

For the crab cakes:

1 pound crabmeat
¼ cup mayonnaise

2 tablespoons minced red onion
1½ tablespoons minced peeled apple
1 tablespoon crushed red pepper flakes
1 teaspoon shredded lemon zest
2 teaspoons freshly squeezed lemon juice
1 teaspoon chopped parsley
¼ teaspoon freshly ground black pepper
2 egg yolks
Pinch of salt
½ cup panko bread crumbs
Olive oil

First, make the salad. Whisk together the vinegar and mustard. Drizzle in oil, whisking constantly. Season with salt and pepper and gently toss half of the dressing with the arugula or spinach, adding more dressing as needed to coat lightly.

For the crab cakes, combine all ingredients except the panko, stirring to combine. Stir in ¼ cup of the panko, reserving the rest in a shallow bowl. Form crab cakes into 2-ounce balls, pressing into remaining panko to coat lightly and gently flatten.

Brush a nonstick skillet or griddle with oil and sear cakes over medium-high heat until golden brown on both sides and warmed through.

Serve each crab cake with a cup of the salad.

GIRL & THE GOAT

809 WEST RANDOLPH STREET, WEST LOOP
(312) 492-6262
WWW.GIRLANDTHEGOAT.COM
OWNERS: KEVIN BOEHM AND ROB KATZ
EXECUTIVE CHEF-PARTNER: STEPHANIE IZARD

Before she was a TV celebrity and chef-owner of a restaurant with two-hour-plus wait times, she was one of the youngest restaurant owners in Chicago and a master of seafood cooking. Stephanie Izard opened Scylla—before she even turned thirty—in a quaint little brown house in the Bucktown neighborhood that chef Takashi Yagihashi of Takashi now calls home.

Just after closing the two-year-old restaurant, Izard went on to compete and win Bravo! TV's *Top Chef* season four, during which she also took home the "fan favorite" award for her friendly, agreeable demeanor and big, squinty-eyed smile set between long strands of curly brown hair. At home, she maintains that reputation of fun-seeking friendliness with a quiet calmness in the kitchen that's focused and disciplined at the same time.

And in true Izard fashion, outside of the restaurant, she devotes time to Common Threads, a nonprofit organization dedicated to teaching fresh, healthy cooking and nutrition to inner city children, cofounded by Art Smith, formerly Oprah Winfrey's personal chef, who opened Table 52 in Chicago and Art and Soul in Washington, D.C. Izard even donated the sleek and shiny GE Monogram kitchen she won on *Top Chef* to the organization.

After two years in the making, during which Izard worked to raise additional funds, pair up with the right restaurateurs, battle trademark issues (the original name Drunken Goat was taken by a cheesemaker), and build a following through a traveling underground dinner club, Izard finally opened the heavily anticipated Girl & the Goat, and the crowds poured in. In a modern-day urban "gastropub" dressed in black, slate gray, and wood detailing with an energetic front bar flowing into a vigorous dining room, groups of friends and couples share small plates of Midwestern vegetables, pull-apart house-baked breads, pastas, delicate shellfish, and of course plenty of meat-based dishes.

"For me going out to eat should be about having some drinks and great food and hanging with your friends and having fun," Izard says. "It reminds me of sitting in Italy outside with friends at a big table and sharing a bunch of food and wine and really enjoying the evening."

And, in true gastropub fashion, bartenders take their cocktails just as seriously as the cooks, who work side by side in an open kitchen line with rows upon rows of Mexican terra cotta and ceramic plates stacked loft-ceiling high.

Goat makes an appearance, in the form of goat "belly" with bourbon-poached lobster and crab, creamy liver mousseline with apple mustard, and as a topper for a pizza with local artisanal cheese and rapini. Izard balances out other risk-taking dishes, such as a wood-oven-roasted pig face and a beef tongue, with a popular roasted cauliflower dish topped with pickled peppers, toasty pine nuts, and mint, and other lighter creations that blend the sweet with the smoky, salty, nutty, herbal, and savory in a play on the six tastes. In this goat sausage and mussel combination, lamb sausage can be substituted for a taste that's just as rich and unique against the lighter mussels.

MUSSELS WITH MIGHTY GOAT SAUSAGE, CILANTRO BUTTER, AND BAGNA CAUDA AIOLI
(Serves 4–6; makes about 1 pound sausage)

For the Mighty Goat sausage:

½ pound goat meat, cubed (substitute lamb if goat is unavailable)
1½ ounces pork meat, cubed
1½ ounces pork fatback, cubed
Salt and freshly ground black pepper, to taste
1 teaspoon ground mustard seed
1 teaspoon ground fennel seed
½ teaspoon ground cardamom
½ clove garlic
1½ teaspoons chopped shallot
¼ cup chopped fennel bulb
1 tablespoon white wine
½ tablespoon water
2 teaspoons tamarind paste
2 tablespoons chopped cilantro

For the cilantro butter:

2 cloves garlic
¼ cup chopped cilantro
½ cup butter (1 stick)
Grated zest of 1 orange
½ teaspoon cayenne pepper

For the bagna cauda aioli:

2 egg yolks
1 tablespoon Dijon mustard
1 tablespoon sherry vinegar
1 cup vegetable oil
3 anchovy fillets
3 large garlic cloves, chopped
Salt, to taste

For the mussels:

1 tablespoon olive oil
¼ cup finely chopped shallots
1 pound mussels, cleaned
⅔ cup Goose Island Sofie ale, or other Belgian-style ale
Crushed red pepper, to taste
Salt, to taste
1 cup croutons, packaged or homemade

MODERN GASTROPUB

What started with Hopleaf rolling out a 250-plus craft beer list and a food lover's menu to boot years ago has as of late grown into a sweeping trend across Chicago. Beer and cocktails share center stage with the food at these modern-day "gastropubs," a contemporary rendition of the typical British drinking spots where office workers stop by for happy hour and early—rowdy—group dinners. Except, unlike in London, the food-focused pubs here don't close down pre-midnight. Instead they rage through the night in a perfect blend of cocktail bar and upscale restaurant, a source for after-work drinks, dinners, and late-night noshing.

Stephanie Izard pressed the trend onward with Girl & the Goat, a friends-meeting-friends sharing experience where mixologists, or "bar chefs" as they've come to be called, concentrate on creating classic and cutting-edge cocktails at the bar and the cooks keep up their end of the bargain in the kitchen. The popularity and number of home-based craft breweries, which started with mainstay Goose Island Brewery, have exploded. Revolution Brewing, by former Goose Island master brewers, serves up comfort food in a restaurant that wraps around a central bar. Then there's Metropolitan Brewing and Half Acre, once a brewery-only spot in Lincoln Square, now a brewery-restaurant that leans toward beer-friendly pork dishes. Brewers have also teamed up with chefs at their restaurants for special beer-pairing dinners, and the togetherness continues at major public and private events around the city, even weddings. It seems the gastropub concept has extended beyond the brick and mortar into a cultural "revolution" that's defined Chicagoans' penchant for great food, and great drink.

First, prepare the Mighty Goat sausage. Place the goat meat, pork, and pork fatback on a sheet tray and freeze until cold but not frozen. Season the meat with salt, pepper, mustard seed, fennel seed, and cardamom.

Using a stand mixer fitted with a meat grinder attachment, grind the meat, garlic, shallot, and fennel together into the mixing bowl. On medium speed, emulsify the meat with the wine, water, and tamarind using the paddle attachment, about 3–4 minutes. Cook a small bit of sausage to check for seasoning and adjust if necessary. Mix the cilantro in on low speed until fully incorporated. Cover meat and refrigerate. (This can be made a day ahead.)

Next, prepare the cilantro butter. In a food processor or blender, blend the garlic and cilantro together until smooth. Add the butter, cube by cube, until well combined and aerated. Add the orange zest and pepper powder and continue mixing until blended and aerated.

To make the bagna cauda aioli, in a blender, combine egg yolks, mustard, and vinegar. On medium-high speed, slowly pour the oil in to emulsify and thicken. When emulsified, add the anchovies and garlic and blend until smooth. Season with salt to taste, cover, and refrigerate.

In a large pot with a lid, heat the olive oil and cook shallots over medium heat for 4 minutes. Add goat sausage and cook, breaking up into small pieces, about 3–4 minutes or until slightly browned.

Add the mussels and beer. Cover and steam mussels until all mussels are open, about 2–3 minutes. Discard any mussels that do not open. Add cilantro butter and cook until melted. Season with crushed red pepper and salt. Add croutons and toss to coat and moisten. Transfer mussels to serving bowls. Drizzle bagna cauda aioli over the mussels.

Naha

500 North Clark Street, River North
(312) 321-6242
www.naha-chicago.com
Owners: Carrie and Michael Nahabedian
Executive Chef: Carrie Nahabedian

Before the words "local," "sustainable," and "green" took on the meanings we now know, there was "Carrie." As one of the original board members for Green City Market, Chicago's first-ever open-air farmers' market, founded by Midwestern food expert and cookbook author Abby Mandel (see page 10), Nahabedian, alongside her family, has worked to position Naha as a place for fine-dining-inspired cuisine using the best of Midwestern and seasonal foods in a more informal but chic setting, defined by white marble, dark woods, and a minimalist approach to décor.

Also playing a strong role in Carrie Nahabedian's self-described "fusion" restaurant is her strong Armenian heritage, which blends Mediterranean and Middle Eastern flavors in cooking, as well as the lightness of California cuisine she grew to love while serving as executive chef of the Four Seasons in Santa Barbara and Beverly Hills. In Chicago, Nahabedian also honed her fine-dining style with such legendary chefs and restaurateurs as Jean Banchet of Le Français, Gordon Sinclair (where she worked alongside close friend Charlie Trotter), and Jovan Trboyevic of Le Perroquet. That training has translated into combining contrasting flavors and textures that together work in graceful unison. For one, hand-harvested scallops roasted with vanilla bean, caramelized Belgian endive, bosc pears, and coppa ham. For another, roasted aged Moulard duck breast, sweet Michigan cherries, and local turnips "lacquered" with honey and sorghum alongside duck-fat-fried Rose Finn potatoes in a port and lavender reduction.

Winner of numerous James Beard awards and other high accolades, including a Michelin star, Nahabedian was inducted into the Chicago Culinary Museum's Chefs Hall of Fame on September 22, 2009, an occasion Mayor Richard M. Daley proclaimed "Chef Carrie Nahabedian Day in Chicago." Nahabedian has a presence, both figuratively and literally, with a bubbly personality, loud laugh, and big smile, and a reputation for throwing killer holiday parties (and ten-year-anniversary ones). She also serves as a leader for both up-and-coming and established women chefs in Chicago and around the world, remaining an active member of Les Dames d'Escoffier, an international organization of women culinary leaders.

Not only is Nahabedian known for her strong relationships with Midwestern farmers, she has also sought to "trace the source" of other foods from around the globe, at one time joining fellow Dame and Green City Market board member Sarah Stegner (see Prairie Grass Cafe, page 91) on a trip to Alaska where she visited a small group of family fisheries who catch the halibut she sources for the restaurant. While Alaskan halibut would work just as well in this recipe, here Nahabedian has used salmon from the snowy state's Copper River, paired with Wisconsin-grown mushrooms and local peas.

Copper River Salmon with English Pea Cannelloni and Frothy Mushroom Broth
(Serves 8)

For the mushroom stock:

3 cups mushroom scraps (morel bottoms, porcini peels, oyster mushroom ends, Portobello stems) or, if unavailable, 3 pounds button mushrooms
2 cups white wine
4 cups water
3 tablespoons salt

For the cannelloni pasta sheets:

3 eggs
9 ounces all-purpose flour
Pinch of salt
Olive oil for coating

For the cannelloni filling:

4 ounces mascarpone cheese, softened
1 cup cooked peas
1 egg
½ cup grated Parmesan cheese
Salt and freshly ground pepper to taste

For the mushrooms, mushroom froth, salmon, and plating:

¼ cup unsalted butter
1 pound fresh morel mushrooms, cleaned
Salt and freshly ground black pepper to taste
⅓ cup half-and-half
⅓ cup skim milk
Olive oil
8 4-ounce pieces sockeye salmon fillet
½ pound fresh pea tendrils
1 large or 2 medium black truffles (optional)

For the mushroom stock, combine all ingredients in stockpot. Bring to a boil over high heat. Lower heat; simmer until reduced by half. Strain through a mesh strainer without pushing on mushroom pieces. Store in the refrigerator up to 5 days or freeze for future use.

For the cannelloni pasta sheets, make a well in the flour; add the eggs and salt. Mix ingredients with your fingers. Once combined, begin kneading until the dough is smooth, elastic, and not sticky. Cover with plastic wrap; let rest 1 hour. Roll pasta into 2-inch-diameter log. With the heel of your hand, flatten the dough firmly so it can be easily manipulated into the pasta sheeter machine. Using flour as needed, feed the long pasta sheet through the pasta maker, number by number. After the pasta has passed through the smallest setting, cut it into eight 5 x 3½-inch pasta sheets. Cook the pasta in rapidly boiling salted water just until barely tender. Transfer to ice water to stop the cooking and then coat lightly in oil.

Preheat the oven to 400°F. For the cannelloni filling, place mascarpone in a large mixing bowl. In a food processor, puree peas, egg, and cheese. Stir puree into mascarpone; add salt and pepper to taste.

On each pasta sheet, spoon a line of filling across the 5-inch side, an inch in from the edge. Roll tightly, not letting the filling squeeze out the ends. Place seam side down on a buttered baking sheet with ½-inch sides. Add water to cookie sheet so cannelloni do not burn on the bottom. Bake until ends are golden brown and filling has expanded. Remove to a warm place, but leave oven on.

Meanwhile, cook the butter in a sauté pan over medium-low heat until lightly browned and fragrant, being careful not to burn. Add the morels, cook until softened. Season with salt and pepper; set aside.

Heat 1 cup of the mushroom stock with half-and-half and skim milk. Bring to a gentle boil, check seasoning, and adjust if necessary.

Heat a thin film of olive oil in an ovenproof sauté pan until hot. Season salmon with salt and pepper to taste. Cook salmon, skin side up 2–3 minutes to brown; flip. Transfer to 400°F oven; roast to desired doneness, about 4-5 minutes for medium.

Divide pea tendrils evenly in eight shallow bowls. Place 1 cannelloni in each bowl; top with a salmon fillet. Reheat the morels; spoon over salmon. Froth the mushroom stock with a hand blender. Spoon froth over morels as a sauce, frothing stock again as needed. Shave truffles over the top, if desired and if available.

Les Nomades

222 East Ontario Street, River North
(312) 649-9010
www.lesnomades.net
Owner: Mary Beth Liccioni
Former Executive Chef: Chris Nugent

Les Nomades is the type of place where young couples get engaged, and others celebrate their anniversaries. A quiet enclave tucked in the center of bustling River North, the fine-dining French institution has a penchant for the romantic, and for chef stardom. On the outside, a small garden almost hides the cottage of a building, ivy trickling up the vintage façade. Inside, it's as cozy and antiquated as a grandmother's home, but with the European charm and subtle elegance you'd expect—embroidered drapes, soft carpeting, white linen, a log-burning fireplace.

Mary Beth Liccioni, a chef and renowned fine-dining restaurateur, mans the door just as she always has, kindly greeting regulars and newcomers alike. First co-owner with former husband and chef Roland Liccioni, who has since departed for other endeavors, she now entirely owns the famed restaurant, originally developed by Jovan Trboyevic, who also belongs to this "old guard" of fine dining in Chicago.

Enter chef Chris Nugent: the new guard. Trained by Rick Tramonto, Michael Kornick, and other icons, Nugent helped continue Les Nomades' tradition of classic French cuisine but brought to the table his own creative tricks and whimsical plating style. He also deepened Les Nomades' focus on classic Midwestern foods, from hunter's meats like squab and venison to small-farmer produce like ramps and baby asparagus in the spring, heirloom tomatoes and blueberries in the summer, and squashes of all shapes and sizes in the fall.

That myriad of squashes makes its way into his recipe below, paired with what else but romantic, succulent, indulgent lobster: a close representation of the Les Nomades institution itself. His favored kabocha squash, also known as a Japanese pumpkin, is a winter squash with a knobby, dark green shell and supersweet fleshy interior that's bright yellow-orange. Sweeter than butternut squash, in taste it most resembles pumpkin and sweet potatoes. Substitute buttercup, turban squash, or pie pumpkin if kabocha is hard to find. Alba mushrooms, also referred to as clamshell or beech mushrooms, have a delicate shellfish taste and creamy white caps atop thin stems. Substitute oyster mushrooms, cut into thin slices, if alba mushrooms are not available.

Though Nugent is no longer at Les Nomades, he continues his refined, innovative renditions of Midwestern seasonal classics at his restaurant, Goosefoot, in the Lincoln Square neighborhood.

Herb Roasted Maine Lobster with Winter Squash Mosaic, Alba Mushrooms, and Curry Brown Butter Emulsion

(Serves 6)

For the kabocha squash puree:

1 medium kabocha squash
½ teaspoon ground cinnamon
¼ teaspoon ground nutmeg
2 tablespoons clover honey
3 tablespoons unsalted butter
Salt, to taste

For the spaghetti squash:

1 medium spaghetti squash, halved lengthwise,
   seeded
1 teaspoon caraway seeds
2 tablespoons garlic oil
2 teaspoons minced chives
Salt and freshly ground black pepper, to taste

For the Parisienne squash:

1 acorn squash, halved crosswise, seeded
1 teaspoon thinly sliced sage leaves
¼ teaspoon ground cinnamon
¼ teaspoon ground nutmeg
1 teaspoon brown sugar
¼ teaspoon Madras curry powder
2 tablespoons unsalted butter
Salt, to taste

For the lobster:

3 1-pound live lobsters
2 tablespoons unsalted butter
2 tablespoons lemon juice
Salt, to taste

For the curry brown butter emulsion:

Reserved lobster shells
¼ cup olive oil
2 cups diced white onion
½ cup diced celery
½ cup diced carrot
½ cup diced fennel
3 cloves garlic, sliced
1 tablespoon tomato paste
¼ cup brandy
½ cup white wine
5 cups chicken stock
1 teaspoon coriander seeds
½ teaspoon fennel seeds
2 sprigs fresh tarragon
1 bay leaf
1 kaffir lime leaf
½ teaspoon Madras curry powder
Pinch of cayenne pepper
½ cup heavy cream
½ cup coconut milk
¼ cup unsalted butter

For the herb crust:

½ cup chopped Italian parsley
¼ cup chopped fresh basil
1 clove garlic, peeled
1 cup panko breadcrumbs
Salt, to taste

For the mushrooms:

2 teaspoons unsalted butter
1 tablespoon olive oil
¼ cup alba mushrooms, cleaned and quartered
2 teaspoons minced shallots
½ teaspoon minced garlic
1 teaspoon fresh thyme leaves
¼ cup thinly sliced baby spinach
Salt and freshly ground black pepper, to taste

For the garnish:

2 ounces fresh pea tendrils

First, prepare the three squashes. Preheat oven to 325°F. Roast kabocha squash and spaghetti squash on separate sheet pans, cut side down, covered with foil. Check spaghetti squash after 45 minutes. If skin is tender and meat is fleshy, remove squash, continuing to roast the kabocha squash another 15–20 minutes, or until skin and flesh are tender. Cool both squashes to room temperature.

Using a fork, carefully scrape out the spaghetti squash strands into a bowl, season with caraway seeds, garlic oil, chives, salt, and pepper, toss lightly, and set aside. Scoop kabocha squash into a food processor, add cinnamon, nutmeg, honey, butter, and salt, and puree until smooth, about 2–3 minutes. Set aside.

To prepare the Parisienne squash, scoop flesh from acorn squash using a Parisienne scoop or small melon baller. Heat a small sauté pan over medium heat, add squash and remaining ingredients, and sauté until squash is tender, about 4 minutes. Set aside.

Next, begin preparing the lobsters. Separate each into tail, large claws, and small claws. In a large stockpot bring water to a boil over high heat. Add the lobster tails, cook for 2 minutes, then add the large claws, cook for 1 minute, and finally add the small claws and cook 4 additional minutes for a total of 7 minutes. Drain lobster and transfer to a basin of ice water to stop the cooking. When cool enough to handle, crack lobster shells, carefully remove the meat, cut each tail into six slices, and set lobster meat aside. Reserve shells for the next step.

To make the curry brown butter emulsion, heat the olive oil over medium-high heat in a large, heavy-bottomed saucepan. Add lobster shells and sauté for 4 minutes. Add onion, celery, carrots, fennel, and garlic and sauté until vegetables are soft, about 6 minutes. Add tomato paste and caramelize, about 3 minutes. Deglaze pan with brandy and white wine, and cook until reduced by half. Add chicken stock, coriander seeds, fennel seeds, bay leaf, kaffir lime leaf, curry powder, and cayenne pepper. Simmer for 45 minutes. Strain mixture, discarding solids. Return sauce to pan and reduce to 1 cup. Add cream and coconut milk. In a small saucepan over medium-low heat, melt butter. Cook, stirring often, until butter turns an amber brown. Emulsify butter into curry sauce with a handheld immersion blender. Set aside.

To prepare the herb crust, place all ingredients in a food processor, processing until finely ground. Set aside. Turn oven up to 400°F.

To prepare the mushrooms, heat butter and oil in a medium sauté pan over medium-high heat. Add the mushrooms, shallots, garlic, and thyme and sauté 2 minutes. Add spinach and continue to cook until just wilted. Season with salt and pepper and set aside.

To finish the lobster, melt the butter in an ovenproof sauté pan over medium-high heat. Cook until butter just begins to brown. Add lobster meat and sprinkle with herb crust and salt. Cook 1 minute, transfer pan to the oven, and bake 2 minutes. Remove pan from oven, add lemon juice, and keep warm.

To serve, draw a line of the kabocha squash puree down the center of six warm plates. On one side, place a small spoonful of the alba mushroom mixture and top with three slices of lobster tail. On the other side, place a spoonful of the spaghetti squash and top with lobster. Arrange Parisienne squash on the plate and spoon brown butter emulsion over and around lobster. Garnish with pea tendrils.

Yoshi's Café

3257 North Halsted Street, Lakeview
(773) 248-6160
www.yoshiscafe.com
Chef-Owners: Yoshi and Nobuko Katsumura

When Asian "fusion" picked up in popularity on the West Coast in the early nineties, there was Yoshi's in Chicago. The charming white stone building with the distinctive blue awning has stood strong for more than two decades on this strip of East Lakeview, once a much grittier, rougher neighborhood than the family-friendly, gay-friendly collection of residents and restaurants it is now.

Yoshi Katsumura and his wife Nobuko dared to depart from the traditional Japanese sushi route, melding fine French cooking techniques with Asian flavors and textures far off anyone's culinary radar at the time they opened. Katsumura has continued to build his reputation for eclectic haute cuisine, bringing in Italian, contemporary American, and other

foods, in such combinations as a tartare of hamachi (amberjack) with guacamole, Japanese halibut with a classic French fish fumet and cream sauce, Japanese kabocha pumpkin ravioli, grilled tofu steak with brie and basil, and one of the first wagyu beef burgers in town before the trend hit citywide.

Once known for special occasions, fine dining, and romantic white-tablecloth dinners, Yoshi's switched to a lighter, more casual cafe of a place about a decade ago, still with the emphasis on seafood and a refined, eclectic menu, but more opened up, with new tiled floors and a touch more noise and life. One thing that didn't change: the sight of Yoshi and Nobuko table-hopping to talk to the die-hard core of regulars as well as the newcomers. Their hospitality and warmth, aside from just the food, have helped Yoshi's weather the ups and downs of the restaurant industry over the years and adapt to the times.

OVEN-ROASTED LAKE SUPERIOR WHITEFISH WITH MANILA CLAMS AND DASHI BROTH
(Serves 2)

1 tablespoon olive oil, divided
¼ teaspoon sea salt
¼ teaspoon freshly ground black pepper
3 tablespoons all-purpose flour
2 6–8-ounce whitefish fillets (if unavailable, use cod)
1 vine-ripened or plum tomato, seeded and diced
½ cup snow peas
1 cup bonito fish stock (dashi)
1 tablespoon soy sauce
10 Manila clams
½ teaspoon chopped fresh chives

Preheat oven to 450°F.

Heat ½ tablespoon oil in an oven-safe skillet over medium-high heat. In a shallow bowl, mix together salt, pepper, and flour. Lightly dredge fish fillets in flour, shaking to remove excess. Add fish, skin side up, to the pan and cook until browned, about 1–2 minutes. Flip the fish and roast in the oven, skin side down, for 5–7 minutes or until opaque.

Remove fish from pan, set aside. Add the remaining oil to the pan along with the tomato and snow peas. Cook vegetables until slightly softened, 2 minutes. Set aside.

In a separate frying pan or pot, bring fish stock and soy sauce to a simmer over medium-high heat. Add Manila clams, cover, and steam until shells open, about 1–2 minutes.

To serve, divide vegetables evenly between two deep bowls and top each with a fish fillet. Slowly pour in fish stock, and then add the clams. Garnish with chives.

LULA CAFÉ

2537 NORTH KEDZIE BOULEVARD, LOGAN SQUARE
(773) 489-9554
WWW.LULACAFE.COM
EXECUTIVE CHEFS–OWNERS: JASON HAMMEL AND AMALEA TSHILDS

It's the year 2000. The Y2K horrors didn't happen, but the dot-com boom has busted. A new president will head the country after a hotly contested election. And in Chicago, a new wave of modern American restaurants have opened or are about to open. They're sustainable, local, and seasonally focused, but those words aren't even in the picture yet.

As part of this "first wave" led by the likes of Bruce Sherman, Carrie Nahabedian, Sarah Stegner, and Paul Kahan, the chef duo Jason Hammel and Amalea Tshilds began their partnerships with Midwestern farmers and producers to open a restaurant that would stand as more casual and approachable than the Blackbirds, Nahas, and North Ponds of the world, but would still focus as heavily on cooking with the seasons and harvesting the best this country's region had to offer. Enter, Lula Café.

Minimalist, yet fresh and airy, Lula began as a twenty-some-seat BYOB eatery in the heart of the slightly rough Logan Square neighborhood that's just now the new hipster hotspot. The husband-wife team quickly proved that creative and refined market-driven cuisine didn't have to be consumed in a traditional three- or four-star space, though they've earned that many stars in national critics' rankings. Since then, they've expanded the Lula space to include more seats at the bar, on the patio, and at the back of the house near the pastry kitchen where a prize recent recruit, veteran pastry chef Kate Neumann, builds her artistic desserts. Outside the restaurant, Hammel and Tshilds together remain an integral part of the city's farmers' markets and many educational initiatives and events focused on issues of sustainability and food production.

"This recipe imagines a border between Spain and Italy, a place I wish existed," Hammel says. "It's a dish we came up with in March, when it was still cold and we were forced to turn toward the pantry. White asparagus can be a good choice in the spring when you're impatient for green, tired of root vegetables and looking for something bright, acidic, and crunchy to put you in an elevated mood. Lightly pickling the asparagus matches the 'cooking from the pantry' ethos of this dish."

At Lula, chefs will first poach the fish *sous vide* at low temperatures using a fennel-scented, milky broth. Home cooks, however, can baste the fish to imitate the gentle and constant heat and moisture of a *sous vide* bath. The poaching liquid may be prepared ahead, cooled, and stored for a few days. Remember to store asparagus in water, Hammel says, with a halved lemon to prevent oxidation.

Milk-Poached Cod with White Asparagus, Charred Piquillo Peppers, and Lemon-Fennel Risotto

(Serves 4)

For the poaching liquid, cod, and piquillo peppers:

2 tablespoons unsalted butter
2 fennel bulbs, cored and thinly sliced
1 cup Pernod, absinthe, or anise-flavored liqueur
 (such as Herbsaint)
½ cup sugar
1 cup chicken stock or low-sodium broth
1 cup whole milk
¼ teaspoon salt
4 5-ounce cod fillets
1 8-ounce can piquillo peppers, drained

For the asparagus salad:

1 bunch white asparagus, bottom ends trimmed
 and stalks peeled
¼ cup sugar
½ cup lemon juice
½ cup extra-virgin olive oil
2 tablespoons champagne vinegar
1 bulb fennel, cored and shaved using a
 vegetable peeler
½ tablespoon chopped fresh dill

For the risotto:

3 quarts chicken stock or low-sodium chicken
 broth
2 tablespoons butter
2 tablespoons olive oil
2 yellow onions, minced
1 bulb fennel, cored and minced
Zest of 2 lemons
1 teaspoon fennel seeds, toasted and crushed
4 cups Arborio rice (just under 2 pounds)
¼ bottle dry white wine (a generous ¾ cup)

In a heavy-bottomed saucepan, melt the butter over medium heat. Add fennel and cook until caramelized, about 5 minutes. Reduce heat to medium-low if butter begins to brown too fast. Add the Pernod, sugar, and stock or broth. Bring to a boil, then turn off heat immediately, allowing to cool slightly. Stir in milk, season with salt, and cool completely. Set aside.

For the asparagus salad, blanch asparagus in salted boiling water until just tender. Transfer to an ice bath. Drain, slice into ¼-inch-thick pieces, and set aside. In a large bowl, mix together the sugar, lemon juice, oil, and vinegar. Fold in asparagus, shaved fennel, and dill. Refrigerate.

Blister the piquillo peppers on an open flame or in a broiler. Cut into ½-inch-thick slices. Set aside.

For the risotto, bring the stock in a large stockpot to a gentle simmer over medium-high heat. In a separate large, heavy-bottomed pot over medium-low heat, melt the butter and oil. Add onions, fennel, zest, and fennel seed; cook until soft and translucent. Add the rice and toast until mixture is fragrant and glossy, about 5 minutes.

Add a splash of olive oil if mixture sticks to the pan. Add the wine and bring to a strong simmer, stirring constantly. Continue to cook until almost fully reduced. Pour in the simmering stock, 1 cup at a time, stirring constantly in one direction and maintaining a strong simmer. Allow rice to fully absorb each cup of stock before adding the next. Continue to stir until rice is creamy but still al dente, about 22 minutes. Set aside. If any stock remains, cool and refrigerate for other use.

To prepare the cod, bring the poaching liquid back up to a simmer over medium-high heat. Reduce heat to medium, bringing liquid down to a gentle simmer. Carefully add fillets and poach until fish is opaque and just cooked through, about 3 minutes.

To serve, spoon the risotto evenly on one half of each of four plates. On the other half of the plate, add a spoonful of the sliced piquillo peppers, warmed in the microwave for 10–20 seconds. Place a cod fillet over the peppers. Ladle about 1 ounce of the poaching liquid over the fish. Serve with asparagus salad in individual, chilled bowls.

Nightwood

2119 South Halsted Street, Pilsen
(312) 526-3385
WWW.NIGHTWOODRESTAURANT.COM
Executive Chefs–Owners: Jason Hammel and Amalea Tshilds
Chef de Cuisine: Jason Vincent

At Jason Hammel and Amalea Tshilds's second outpost, Jason Vincent runs the day-to-day kitchen and frequently changing menu, continuing in the tradition of seasonal, market-fresh cuisine that the husband-wife duo began more than a decade ago. Vincent also brings a butchering artistry to the game, bringing in whole hogs and even entire sides of beef from Midwestern farms to explore new cuts, tastes, and menu adventures while reducing waste at the same time, an important part of the sustainable, Slow Food philosophy of protecting and preserving the earth and its creatures to which the entire restaurant team subscribes.

Vincent also shows a finesse with seafood at this Lula sibling that's just as casual, earthy, and outdoorsy, thanks to a similar minimalist design with natural woods and a breezy in-and-out patio with doors that open during the warmer months. The main difference? Cocktails and wine are available here, and they're just as integrated with the market-fresh approach— mixologists use what's in season for both classic and creative concoctions, matched by an approachable yet well-thought-out wine list.

Yet another difference between Nightwood and Lula Café is Vincent's outright embrace of Midwestern classics, exemplified by his modernized recipe here that plays off the classic and hearty bacon-based chowders and smoked trout fillets of Wisconsin's central farms and Lake Michigan shores. Serving the bacon garnish only partially cooked, Vincent says, helps "melt" the smoky meat as it continues to cook in the hot soup.

Wisconsin Trout Soup with Potato-Infused Cream and Bacon
(Serves 4)

For the soup:

3 slices bacon, diced
1 small yellow onion, chopped
1 celery rib, chopped
½ bulb fennel, cored, chopped
Salt and pepper
1 head garlic, cloves peeled and thinly sliced
½ teaspoon tomato paste
1 cup dry white wine
Splash of orange juice
Splash of apple cider (optional)

1 12–14-ounce smoked trout fillet
4 cups fish, chicken, or vegetable stock or
   low-sodium broth
¼ cup chopped fresh chives, divided
1 cup sour cream or crème fraîche

For the potato cream and cheese garnish:

1 cup heavy cream
3 small fingerling or other starchy potatoes
   about the size of an index finger
½ cup grated Wisconsin or other artisanal,
   good-quality sharp cheddar cheese

In a heavy-bottomed nonaluminum pot over low heat, cook the bacon pieces until some of the fat has rendered but pieces are not crisp, about 2–3 minutes. Transfer bacon pieces with a slotted spoon to paper towels; set aside.

Turn heat up to medium. Add the onion, celery, and fennel and cook until vegetables are soft and translucent but not browned, stirring constantly, about 2 minutes. Season with salt and pepper. Add the garlic and cook until fragrant, 30 seconds. Add the tomato paste and continue to stir, 30 seconds. Pour in the wine, orange juice, and apple cider if using, stirring to combine. Cook until liquid has fully reduced and mixture is dry. Add the trout flesh and head, stock, and half of the chives.

Bring mixture to a gentle simmer. Continue to simmer, uncovered, skimming foam, not the fat, off the surface several times.

Meanwhile, prepare the potato cream garnish. Heat the cream in a small saucepan over medium heat. Bundle the potatoes in cheesecloth and submerge in the cream. Continue to cook until cream reduces by a third and is thick enough to coat the back of a spoon. Using a wooden spoon, smash the potatoes slightly. Remove the potato bundle and set aside. Transfer saucepan with the cream to an off burner. Whisk in a touch of water if cream becomes gluey.

Soup will be ready when broth is clearer, mildly salty and fishy in taste but smooth and rich, about 45 minutes to 1 hour. Remove from heat, allow to cool slightly. Add the sour cream or crème fraîche and stir constantly to thicken, about 3 minutes.

Transfer soup to a blender in small batches and puree until smooth. Alternatively, puree soup using an immersion blender. Strain soup several times through a very fine strainer until almost smooth. Soup will still have a slightly chalky consistency.

To serve, divide among four bowls. Drizzle each with the warm potato cream. Remove potatoes from bundle; roughly chop. Garnish with chopped potatoes, bacon, remaining chives, and cheddar cheese, if desired.

BAR GIBSONS STEAKS·FISH

HONORARY
★★ FRANK SINATRA ★★ PL

E BELLEVUE PL

N RUSH ST

GIBSONS

BEEF, LAMB, AND MORE

Chicago's reputation as a meat-and-potatoes kind of town began with the stockyards and steakhouses that developed post-fire in the 1900s, and later post–World War II.

But since then, and long before writers Michael Pollan and Eric Schlosser drew our attention to the way animals are raised and harvested in this country, chefs in Chicago were already building relationships with smaller, noncommercial meat producers in Illinois, Iowa, Indiana, and Wisconsin to source not only typical Midwestern hunting game meat but also sustainably produced beef, pork, lamb, and even goat.

Sustainably produced meat means that animals are raised on open pastures and/or fed non-GMO grains and, above all, treated with kindness and respect. Heartland Meats in western Illinois and Dietzler Farms in Wisconsin lead as sustainable beef producers, while Mint Creek Farm is known for its lamb. Sarah Stegner of Prairie Grass Cafe sources Tallgrass beef raised on TV journalist Bill Kurtis's 60,000 acres of grassland, and Stephanie Izard buys pastured goat meat from one of the brothers behind Kilgus Farmstead, a Central Illinois grass-fed dairy farm.

Yet even as meat consumption continues as a tradition in Chicago, many chefs have sought to include more vegetarian and vegan cooking in their repertoire. Most notably, Karyn Calabrese has led the city and, many say, the nation in her "raw" cuisine and her focus on delicious meatless meals, including the vegan "shepherd's pie" included in the pages to come.

Gibsons Bar & Steakhouse

1028 North Rush Street, Gold Coast
(312) 266-8999
WWW.GIBSONSSTEAKHOUSE.COM
Executive Corporate Chef: Randy Waidner
Executive Chef, Rush Street: Dan Huebschmann

Strong martinis with gibson onions and blue cheese olives. A piano player keying Sinatra tunes. Crowds of well-heeled locals, affluent suburbanites, city politicians, sports team players, and the occasional celebrity. Giant-size steaks served rare, with a crackly crust.

Gibsons is old-school Chicago at its best. A classic steakhouse, the restaurant harkens back to the two-martini lunches and power dinners of the fifties and sixties, though the restaurant itself isn't quite that old.

Everyone wants a seat in the wood-floored main dining room, packed with leather booths and waiters wearing white coats and black ties. It's loud, clubby, and the place to see and be seen. Major business deals are made here. Jack Nicholson declares it his favorite spot in the city. Pictures of other famous patrons from the past and present line the walls leading to the upstairs banquet area, where Mayor Richard M. Daley hosted scores of private events.

Randy Waidner had big shoes to fill when he joined the team on the heels of a chef who ran the kitchen for the last decade. But Waidner has both maintained Gibsons' high standards and breathed new life into the place. Many farm visits and phone calls later, Waidner's proud of leading the company's switch to PM Beef in Minnesota, a beef supplier sourcing from a network of small family farms within 100 miles of its headquarters. These farms are also strict about the welfare of their animals and their impact on the environment; many have experimented with energy-saving equipment and technologies.

While the Gibsons menu has remained unchanged for years, Waidner spreads his creative wings at private events and monthly wine dinners. This tartare recipe continues to steal that show.

Prime Beef Tartare with Quail Egg Salad and Savory Dijon Ice Cream
(Serves 4)

For the savory Dijon ice cream:

1 cup heavy cream
½ cup milk
¼ teaspoon curry powder
¼ teaspoon vanilla extract
Pinch of kosher salt
3 egg yolks
½ cup packed light brown sugar
3 tablespoons Dijon mustard

For the beef tartare:

5 ounces prime beef fillet
2 teaspoons chopped fresh chives
1 teaspoon chopped fresh parsley
1 teaspoon chopped cornichon pickle
1 teaspoon chopped capers
$1/8$ teaspoon kosher salt
$1/8$ teaspoon freshly ground black pepper
1 tablespoon extra-virgin olive oil
1 tablespoon ketchup

For the quail egg salad:

1 tablespoon extra-virgin olive oil
1 teaspoon freshly squeezed lemon juice
⅛ teaspoon kosher salt
⅛ teaspoon freshly ground black pepper
2 cups baby arugula
4 quail eggs, hard-boiled, peeled, and quartered
12 slices toasted pretzel baguette

To make the ice cream, bring cream, milk, curry powder, vanilla, and salt just to a boil in a heavy saucepan, stirring occasionally. Meanwhile, whisk together yolks and brown sugar in a large metal bowl until thick and creamy. Add hot cream mixture in a slow stream, whisking constantly.

Pour mixture back into pan. Cook over medium-low heat, stirring constantly with a wooden spoon, until custard is thick enough to coat the back of a metal spoon and registers 170°F on an instant-read thermometer (do not let boil). Remove from heat.

Pour custard through a fine-mesh sieve into a clean metal bowl set over a larger bowl of ice to cool. Whisk in mustard, then continue to chill, stirring occasionally, until cold.

Freeze custard in an ice cream maker according to manufacturer's instructions. Transfer to an airtight container and freeze until firm.

Place the beef in the freezer for 30 minutes to firm up. Mince the beef and mix with the remaining eight tartare ingredients. Refrigerate.

At serving time, whisk together oil, lemon juice, salt, and pepper in a medium bowl. Add arugula, toss lightly. Divide tartare among four plates and top each mound with about 1 tablespoon ice cream. Spoon salad alongside the tartare and top salad with eggs. Garnish each plate with three baguette slices.

CLASSIC CHICAGO STEAKHOUSES

Steakhouses, traditionally considered the fabric of the Chicago restaurant scene, once served as the only type of upscale restaurant open in the city. Shrimp cocktail and oysters on the half shell, giant-size bloodrare and crusty slabs of meat, cheesy twice-baked potatoes, and creamy green spinach—these were and still are the dishes that made these clubby eateries popular during the fifties and sixties when veterans of the war reentered the workforce with money to burn and a strong penchant for cocktailing. Some of the older steakhouses, such as Gene & Georgetti's, once boasted a reservation system as political and tight as a bookie, with celebrities and socialites vying for "the" table to see and be seen.

Classic steakhouses still abound in Chicago, but many have graduated to a more modern feel, such as David Burke's Primehouse (see page 101), which looks to contemporary décor, a chef-driven menu, and creative cocktails for spin on the old

PRAIRIE GRASS CAFE

601 SKOKIE BOULEVARD, NORTHBROOK
(847) 205-4433
WWW.PRAIRIEGRASSCAFE.COM
CHEF-OWNERS: SARAH STEGNER AND GEORGE BUMBARIS

Sarah Stegner and George Bumbaris are a team. For a decade they raised the Ritz Carlton Dining Room to untold heights. And there, the start of the Slow Food movement in Chicago began.

Stegner has served as one of the founding board members of Chicago's Green City Market, the brainchild of her close friend Abby Mandel, who passed away just before the market was ten years old and had grown from five farms to more than fifty. Set in central Lincoln Park, GCM is a second home to Stegner, who roams the stands early every week, checking out the season's best picks. "I believe the food we source locally is always the freshest, and always tastes the best, above everything else," she says.

The Stegner-Bumbaris team took that philosophy one step further by tracing other foods to the source, including those beyond the Illinois border. After tasting TV journalist Bill Kurtis's grass-fed Tallgrass beef, they quickly incorporated it into their menu at the Ritz. Later they made many pilgrimages to the sixty-acre ranch in Kansas, bringing back not just beef but also inspiration for the name of their first restaurant in the northern suburbs. They even used footage of the ranch's tall "prairie grass" stirring in the wind as a live décor. Stegner has also traveled as far as Alaska to trace the source of the halibut she serves, forging lifelong friendships with families that operate fisheries. At home, she brings in her own family, with pies homemade by her mother.

favorites. And at Gibsons, modernization meant focusing more on locally produced, naturally raised meats, specialty appetizers, and a deepening partnership with sister restaurant Hugo's to offer some of the freshest seafood in the city in addition to steaks. At other spots around the city, getting with the times has meant a paint job here, a carpet removal there, but all in all, the heavy protein-alcohol combination remains as timeless in Chicago as ever.

Grass-Fed Beef Brisket with Pan-Roasted Parsnips

(Serves 10–12)

For the brisket:

1 7–8-pound grass-fed beef brisket, such as Tallgrass beef
Kosher salt and freshly ground black pepper, to taste
3 tablespoons olive oil, divided
4 cups diced onions
1 cup peeled and diced carrots
1 cup chopped celery
2 tablespoons minced garlic
1 28-ounce can diced tomatoes, drained
4 bay leaves
4 sprigs fresh thyme
8 cups chicken broth or stock
½ cup packed brown sugar
2 tablespoons unsalted butter

For the parsnips:

10 parsnips, peeled and cut into wedges
2 tablespoons unsalted butter
Kosher salt and freshly ground pepper, to taste

Preheat the oven to 350°F. Season both sides of the meat with salt and pepper. Heat 2 tablespoons of the oil in a large ovenproof sauté pan or roasting pan over medium-high heat and sear brisket to form a crust, about 3–4 minutes per side. Remove from pan.

Add remaining 1 tablespoon oil to the pan and sauté the onions, carrots, and celery until onions are translucent, but not browned, about 2–3 minutes. Add the garlic and cook 1 minute more. Stir in the tomatoes and add the bay leaf, thyme, broth, and brown sugar. Bring to a simmer. Return brisket to pan, cover tightly with lid or heavy-duty foil, and roast for 3½–4 hours or until meat is fork tender.

Blanch parsnips for 3–4 minutes in salted boiling water until tender. Heat butter in a large sauté pan over medium heat. Drain parsnips, add to pan, and sauté until golden brown on all sides and caramelized, about 5–6 minutes.

Remove the brisket from the liquid and set aside to cool slightly. Strain the liquid through a fine-mesh sieve into a medium saucepan, discarding solids. Bring liquid to a boil, turn off heat, and stir in butter.

Slice the brisket against the grain into ¼-inch-thick pieces and arrange on a platter or in individual ceramic bowls. Pour sauce over brisket and serve alongside pan-roasted parsnips.

In no other city will you see a river dyed green in honor of St. Patrick's Day. To say the Irish-American holiday is a big deal in Chicago is an understatement. Just as the day brings with it its share of revelry and, dare one say it, debauchery, St. Patrick's Day also brings together families and friends from all parts of the city, no matter their ethnic background. Downtown, parents and children and adults of all ages flock to Grant Park to watch decorated floats roll down scenic Columbus Drive just off the lake. Further south, the South Side Irish Parade in Beverly that was a longtime tradition sadly ended recently because of issues with crowd control.

Unfortunately, the parade's discontinuance comes largely from Beverly outsiders causing a ruckus in this respectful, family-oriented neighborhood filled with firefighters, police officers, and other hardworking city residents. Beverly, located on the far southwestern edge of Chicago's city limits, has a long-standing Irish component, with not just the yearly parade but a host of Irish pubs, Catholic parishes, and even a replica of an Irish castle built in the late nineteenth century that now houses a church and preschool. The Beverly branch of the Chicago Public Library system also has the largest Irish literature and history collection in the city.

Chicago emerged as the fourth-largest Irish city in America by 1860, just thirty years after the first wave of immigrants flooded into the city, according to the *Encyclopedia of Chicago*, a collection of history produced by the Chicago History Museum, the Newberry Library, and Northwestern University. Out of all these cities, Chicago's Irish in particular flourished, starting off in hard-labor jobs at the city's stockyards, railroads, and steel mills and later moving into higher levels of city government, particularly the police and fire departments, the public school system, and the Roman Catholic archdiocese. Chicago has a strong Catholic contingent apart from the Irish, with many historic, aesthetically beautiful churches scattered throughout the city and a network of parishes that have helped propel this immigrant class upward in both power and influence.

Perhaps the most prominent Irish family is the Daley family, with Richard J. Daley leading Chicago toward big-city status and son Mayor Richard M. Daley securing Chicago's reputation as a clean, vibrant cultural and culinary metropolis. The Democratic political "machine," made up of Irish-Americans as well as Chicagoans of all races,

ethnicities, religions, and heritages, and powered by the city's entrenched network of labor unions, has proved itself a system that "works," but one also rife with contention and controversy.

As the memorable line from the film *The Fugitive* goes, "If they [city government] can dye the river green today [St. Patrick's Day], why can't they dye it blue the other 364 days of the year?" No city can be perfect, after all.

The Drawing Room

937 North Rush Street, Gold Coast
(312) 266-2694
www.thedrchicago.com
Owner: Three Headed Productions
Executive Chef: Nick Lacasse
Chief Mixologist: Charles Joly

It's Thursday night and the first hungry diners have taken their seats at the bar for the once-a-month cocktail-paired dinner. When chef Nick Lacasse and chief mixologist Charles Joly decided to team up for the first event, they built the five-course menu around a New Orleans theme—Lacasse with tender crawfish over creamy grits and later rockfish in browned butter, Joly with rye-based cocktails like the Sazerac and the old-fashioned just as the pre-Prohibition era in cocktailing was making its way back to mixologists' shakers.

The Drawing Room has managed to hold its own, drawing a completely different crowd than the barely legal Privét next door. When it's late night here, the vibe is chill, with couples and small groups cozily huddled in velvet-soft chairs over rocks glasses and candles while bartenders bring loaded carts tableside for old-school mixing.

A number of mixologists have trained here, moving on to compete in national competitions and train other up-and-coming craftmakers. And in the kitchen, Lacasse has managed to do what few other chefs have—taking over a lesser-known kitchen in a quiet, below-ground reservoir and putting his own stamp on the place, making a name for himself.

A protégé of Green Zebra's Shawn McClain, Lacasse shows a similar refinement and respect for quality and in some cases obscure ingredients, but is a little more playful, with no fear of experimentation. Lacasse, unlike many other chefs, can try out new combinations of foods and cuisines and produce dishes that are balanced, thoughtful, and delicious—like his recipe below, an idea that came out of a trip to Cornwall and tasting the area's signature pasty, a baked meat pie typically filled with beef, potato, onion, and swede, or rutabaga. Lacasse puts his own sophisticated twist on the meat pie with confit of rabbit, quince stewed in Riesling, and mint oil, an English condiment. Of course, the dish wouldn't have The Drawing Room's stamp on it without a paired cocktail by Joly, who developed the drink with the idea of using some of the leftover quince compote.

"Cornish Pasty" of Confit Rabbit with Spicy Quince Compote, Pickled Fingerlings, and Mint Oil

(Makes 4 pasties)

For the rabbit and curing spices:

¼ cup kosher salt
1 tablespoon each: ground coriander, fennel seed,
   and white pepper, plus more for seasoning
2 rabbit legs, bone in
2 cups rendered duck fat

For the quince compote:

½ bottle Riesling wine
5 cups water, divided
1 cup honey
3 sticks cinnamon
3 sprigs fresh thyme
Juice of ½ lemon
2 fresh quinces

For the fingerlings:

1 pound fingerling potatoes
¼ cup champagne vinegar
3 tablespoons sugar
1 tablespoon red pepper flakes
Pinch of salt

For the mint oil and pasty assembly:

15 sprigs fresh mint, finely chopped
1 cup extra-virgin olive oil
Pinch of salt and freshly ground black pepper
2 sheets puff pastry, thawed
¼ cup butter, melted

First, cure the rabbit. In a small bowl, mix the salt with the coriander, fennel, and pepper. Liberally season the legs with the spice mixture, cover in plastic wrap, and refrigerate to cure for 1 hour.

Rinse legs under cold water, pat dry. In a roasting pan set over two stovetop burners over medium-low heat, bring the duck fat to a light simmer. Carefully lower the rabbit legs into the fat and continue to simmer lightly until meat easily falls away from bone, about 2 hours. Drain fat into a separate stainless steel bowl, discarding bones and setting the meat aside. Allow fat to cool and set aside.

For the spicy quince compote, first prepare the poaching liquid. Bring the Riesling, 4 cups of the water, honey, cinnamon, and thyme to a simmer in a pot over medium heat. In a small bowl, place the lemon juice and remaining 1 cup water. Peel, core, and finely chop the quinces, adding the quince pieces to the lemon water to prevent oxidation. After 30 seconds, drain quince and add to the pot with the poaching liquid. Simmer until fruit is very soft and semitranslucent and most of liquid is reduced to a syrup consistency, about 45 minutes to 1 hour. Remove thyme sprigs and set aside.

Meanwhile, prepare the pickled fingerlings. Slice potatoes into ½-inch disks and simmer lightly in salted water for about 5 minutes. Drain and allow to drip dry in the strainer for an additional 5 minutes. In the same pot used for the potatoes, add the vinegar and dissolve the sugar over medium-high heat, about 3–5 minutes. In a separate bowl, add the potatoes, red pepper flakes, and salt, pour vinegar-sugar mixture over potatoes, and set aside.

To prepare the mint oil, place mint, olive oil, salt, and pepper in a small bowl or ramekin. Stir lightly to combine and set aside.

Before assembling the pasties, shred the cooked rabbit leg meat and drain the fingerlings from the pickling brine. Combine the meat, potatoes, and all but 1 ounce of the quince compote in a medium bowl. Check seasoning, adding extra salt, coriander, fennel seeds, and white pepper as needed. Add two small spoonfuls of the duck fat and mix to combine. Refrigerate or freeze leftover duck fat for later use. Set remaining quince compote aside for cocktail making.

Preheat the oven to 350°F. Cut pastry into 6-inch circles and brush with melted butter. Divide rabbit mixture among the pastry circles, forming a mound in the center of each. Don't overstuff; refrigerate or freeze any extra rabbit for later use. Fold each circle in half, pinching the edges closed with the back of a fork to resemble an empanada. Brush outsides with the remaining melted butter and bake until golden brown and puffy, about 13 minutes. Serve pasties warm, with the mint oil spooned over the top and a side of braised cabbage or other cooked greens.

CHARLES JOLY'S FOODS BEGINNING WITH "Q" PAIRING COCKTAIL
(Makes 1 cocktail)

1½ ounces Hendrick's gin
¾ ounce Cynar
1 ounce spiced quince compote
 (see recipe above)
¾ ounce freshly squeezed lemon juice
Orange-saffron bitters*

In a mixing glass, combine Hendrick's, Cynar, quince, and lemon. Add ice, shake, and strain into a chilled champagne coupe. Add three drops bitters to the top of the cocktail.

Note: If orange-saffron bitters are not available, use traditional Angostura bitters, which have an orange flavor.

Charles Joly vigorously shakes the stainless-steel canister, his Chicago-flag-tattooed arm tightening to reveal a toning from many hours spent training for triathlons.

Sporting a close-cut beard and an old-school bartender's vest, Joly, the multiple-award-winning master mixologist at The Drawing Room, smiles shyly, his voice calm and contained as he describes each drink. But then his eyes start to widen ever so slightly and words come faster as he runs through a short history of the cocktail, from the pre-Prohibition years and beyond.

It's this excitement, this passion, this endless knowledge about the craft of cocktailing that has fueled an ongoing nationwide movement harkening back to the years before 1920–1933, considered the dark ages of cocktail history when alcohol was banned and so was the art of distillery. It took years, decades, for that mastery of spirits production to come back, pushing aside the "bathtub gin and vodka" that came out of Prohibition, Joly says. In fact, we're well past the days of the sickly sweet, gimmicky cocktail that gained popularity in the fifties and sixties and the rum-and-Coke days, since we've made this recent transition back to artisanal liquors, from traditional ryes to smooth bourbons, floral gins, and even vodkas made to higher standards and sometimes from organic grains.

In Chicago and just outside, Koval and North Shore Distillery have brought back this artistry, even introducing new types of absinthe, aquavit, and other boutique spirits. And in Wisconsin, Death's Door Distillery produces vodka, gin, and an unaged whiskey with wheat and juniper berries sustainably grown and harvested by the family farmers at the tip of Door County Peninsula on Washington Island.

Quality liquors like these make a great base for even greater cocktails, from the old-fashioneds, Manhattans, and Sazeracs of the days of yore to the foamy egg-white "fizz" drinks, herbal infusion concoctions, and other classic-meets-modern spinoffs that make these mixologist-driven bars seem more like an alchemist's lab.

At Donnie Madia and Paul Kahan's Violet Hour, Chicago's first modern-day "speakeasy" inspired by the quiet, cell-phone-free lounges in Manhattan, cocktails may take ten to twenty minutes to make, but what comes to the table is as elaborate in execution and presentation as a dish Kahan or his chefs would make at any of his restaurants.

Here creatively named and made cocktails like the Trading Floor (Hayman's Old Tom gin, pineapple, orgeat, Spice Trader syrup, and Peychaud's bitters) and the Willing Hostage (gin, Bonal, Cynar, and orange bitters) plus whiskey-based drinks like the Gun Shop Sazerac (Rittenhouse rye, Maison Surenne cognac, Herbsaint, and bitters) come alongside chef-driven sharable plates like brandade fritters with smoked maple syrup and tapenade, artisanal cheeses, and lamb sausage flatbread.

"This is the violet hour, the hour of hush and wonder, when the affections glow again and valor is reborn . . . when . . . at any moment we may see the unicorn," goes the quote from Bernard DeVoto's *The Hour*, which served as inspiration for this velvet-draped lounge with regal high-backed chairs for extra intimacy and a Parisian-looking bar with antiquated stools, striped boudoir wallpaper, and mirror-backed shelving.

So many lounges, bars, and restaurant bars have followed the Violet Hour, The Drawing Room, and cocktail-focused spots like Andersonville's In Fine Spirits and Logan Square's The Whistler in their emphasis on drink programs. Restaurants and food-focused bars following suit in this way include The Bristol, Graham Elliot, Sepia, Province, Naha, Sable Kitchen + Bar, Gilt Bar, and Maude's Liquor Bar.

Bridget Alpert has a lot to do with this growing group of "bar chefs." A master mixologist and book author, Alpert founded the Academy of Spirits and Fine Service, where Joly and countless other award-winning mixologists, bar managers, and other hospitality professionals in Chicago and beyond learned and honed their craft.

Inside and outside the bar and restaurant doors, many of these cocktail artisans have teamed up with other bartenders as well as chefs to host special pairing dinners and cocktail-focused events. Food and the savory is now as much a part of these drinks as they are a part of traditional dishes, and it's a nod to the refinement of both the culinary scene and the cocktail and nightlife scene in Chicago. Cheers to that.

David Burke's Primehouse

616 North Rush Street, River North
(312) 660-6000
www.davidburke.com
Owner-Proprietor: David Burke
Executive Chef: Rick Gresh

David Burke chose well. Looking to expand his steakhouse empire, the New York–based celebrity chef first opened up shop in Las Vegas and later in Chicago at the swanky brand-new James Hotel.

Burke doubtless had a good number of applicants at his fingertips, but he chose the up-and-coming chef Rick Gresh. A Cleveland native and longtime Chicago resident, Gresh had clocked time at Trio, where Grant Achatz rose in the ranks, as well as at other trendy outlets and hotel properties in the city, even earning the Rising Star distinction from the James Beard Foundation.

Gresh puts his own personal touch on the Burke brand, namely by building relationships with Midwestern farmers to include many local and seasonal foods in the extra-size steak menu. He also includes unusually sophisticated entrees for a steakhouse, such as roasted bone marrow, sweetbreads, and lobster fried rice, as well as replacing traditional creamed spinach with a creamed local Swiss chard, and adding earthy porcini mushrooms to mac and cheese.

Gresh also remains active in his community. He regularly updates his blog, *Time Released Brilliance,* while maintaining a steady following on social media platforms. He's also a regular

at culinary events in the city. This is important, because as a Manhattan icon, David Burke had a lot to prove in a city that already boasted several established steakhouses. Another way Burke has sought to differentiate himself from the competition is through dry-aging his steaks for at least 28 days, up to a whopping 75 for an extra "acquired" taste. In the downstairs dry-aging room where many a tour is held, one wall is made up entirely of red Himalayan rock salt, which helps impart a salt crust to the steaks. The rock salt continues throughout the space upstairs, taking up the wall behind the bar and crushed into pieces for the tableside salt shakers. As a result, David Burke's steakhouse exudes a modern feel that contrasts with the dark and clubby atmosphere prevalent at his competition.

For Gresh's recipe, most butchers should have 28-day-aged steaks, even if not dry-aged. Some upscale steak producers, such as Lawry's in New York and Allen Brothers in Chicago, offer the steak online. David Burke's Black Angus prime steaks come from humanely treated animals raised at Creekstone Farms outside Louisville, Kentucky.

PAN-ROASTED 28-DAY BONE-IN BEEF RIBEYE WITH PORCINI MAC AND CHEESE
(Serves 3)

3 20-ounce 28-day-aged beef ribeye steaks, bone in
Kosher salt and freshly ground black pepper, to taste
2 tablespoons grapeseed or canola oil
¾ pound elbow macaroni
3 cups heavy cream
1 cup fresh porcini mushroom pieces
½ cup mascarpone cheese
¼ cup panko (Japanese bread crumbs)
4 tablespoons Parmesan cheese
3 tablespoons chives, finely chopped

Preheat oven to 400°F. Season steaks with salt and pepper. Heat oil in a large oven-safe sauté skillet over medium-high heat. Sear steaks until they form a deep brown crust, about 5 minutes per side. Continue the cooking in the oven until an internal meat thermometer reads 120°F. Remove steaks from oven and let rest 10–15 minutes. Meat will continue to cook to 130°F for medium-rare doneness.

Bring a large pot of salted water to a boil, add elbow macaroni, and cook a little less than instructed on package, or until almost al dente. Drain pasta and set aside.

In a large sauté pan over medium heat, bring heavy cream up to a boil, add porcini mushrooms, and reduce cream by half. Stir in mascarpone cheese and cook 1 minute more, until well combined. Add pasta to the pan and mix to coat. Season with salt and pepper.

Place pasta in a greased casserole dish. Top with bread crumbs, Parmesan cheese, and chives. Bake until browned on top, about 7 minutes. Serve warm with steaks.

Rockit Bar & Grill / Sunda

Rockit Bar & Grill
22 West Hubbard Street, River North
(312) 645-6000
www.rockitbarandgrill.com

Rockit Bar & Grill Wrigleyville
3700 North Clark Street, Lakeview
(773) 645-4400
www.rockitbarandgrill.com

Sunda
110 West Illinois Street, River North
(312) 644-0500
www.sundachicago.com
Owner-Proprietor: Billy Dec
Executive Chef, Rockit: James Gottwald
Executive Chef, Sunda: Jesse de Guzman

Billy Dec started off as a self-proclaimed "nightclub guy," but he's blossomed into one of the most successful restaurateurs in the city. While still running the successful Underground nightclub that regularly sees stars from around the country on weekend nights, Dec blends bar and high-end restaurant at Rockit on the trendy, bar-lined Hubbard Street in River North. For a food rookie, he came out of the blocks with a bang. Rockit posted lines well out the door for the first two years in business, and continues to draw crowds for its famed Rockit Burger and truffle fries, declared number one by Good Morning America.

Building on this stellar start, Dec expanded the Rockit brand to Wrigleyville, just a stone's throw from Chicago's iconic Wrigley Field, home of the Cubs. Given its location, the two-level space with its phalanxes of flat-screen TVs has become as much a sports-viewing and party-planning destination as a foodie one. Chef James Gottwald shows an unmatched level of consistency in his dishes, which look like "bar food" on paper but come out as stepped-up comfort food, from slow-roasted ribs in a homemade sauce to sunny-side-egg-topped Kobe burgers and sweet potato fries dusted with sugar and spice.

"Our whole concept revolves around the highest grade of food and presentation in a very comfortable environment and comfortable price," Dec says. He hardly has to advertise. Word of mouth works for Dec, as does his celebrity-like presence over all sorts of airwaves, from tweeting regularly about his farmers' market finds to appearing on various TV shows, hosting his own very public events, and speaking at very public others.

Sunda, his second restaurant concept after Rockit, focuses less on the bar and sports and more on higher-end dining with an Asian-Indian-influenced menu.

Rockit Burger with Truffle Fries
(Serves 4)

For the burger:

2 pounds ground Kobe beef

For the date aioli:

8 pitted medjool dates
¼ cup extra-virgin olive oil
4 shallots, thinly sliced
3 tablespoons quick-mixing flour,
    such as Wondra*
½ cup vegetable oil, plus 4 tablespoons
    for grilling
Salt and freshly ground black pepper

For the truffle fries:

1 russet potato, peeled and cut into thin sticks
1 tablespoon chopped parsley
2 tablespoons white truffle oil
¼ teaspoon kosher or sea salt
¼ teaspoon freshly ground black pepper

8 ounces brie cheese
4 onion brioche buns

Shape beef into four thick ½-pound patties. Wrap individual patties tightly in plastic wrap and chill for at least an hour. Alternatively, press each portion into an individual 4-inch ring mold, cover with plastic wrap, press down to remove air, and chill.

Meanwhile, prepare the date aioli and fried shallots. Using a mortar and pestle, crush the dates and slowly pour in olive oil. Continue to crush until well mixed. Set aside.

In a small bowl, toss the shallots with the instant flour. In a medium sauté pan, heat ½ cup of the oil over high heat until hot but not smoking. Add shallots and fry until crispy and golden, about 1–2 minutes. Remove from oil and drain on paper towels.

To make the truffle fries, add the potatoes to the heated oil and fry until crispy golden, about 4 minutes. Drain and toss with parsley, truffle oil, salt, and pepper.

Heat grill to medium-high. Brush patties with the remaining vegetable oil and season both sides generously with salt and pepper. For medium rare, grill patties for about 3–4 minutes a side. Top each patty with a slice of brie, close grill, and cook until cheese has melted, about 1 minute.

In a toaster oven or using the grill, toast the buns. To assemble burgers, spread the bun bottoms evenly with the date aioli, top with fried shallots, add the burgers, and close with bun tops. Serve with truffle fries.

Note: Wondra, a quick-mixing flour developed for lump-free blending in sauces and gravies, has lately been used by chefs to create a lighter, airy breading for frying. If Wondra flour is unavailable, combine 1 cup all-purpose flour with 1½ teaspoons baking powder and ½ teaspoon salt. Use this mixture for the recipe.

Mercat a la Planxa

Blackstone Hotel
638 South Michigan Avenue, South Loop
(312) 765-0524
www.mercatchicago.com
Owner-Proprietor: Jose Garces
Management Group: Sage Restaurant Group
Executive Chef: Jose Garces

In true tapas fashion, Mercat a la Planxa is as colorful in décor, people, and food as its name suggests. Mercat, which means "market" in Catalan, is a direct representation of the bustling markets commonly found in Barcelona and other parts of Catalonia, Spain. That's evident in the wide range of produce, meats, cheeses, grains, and other foods peppering the menu as well as in the magentas, fuchsias, reds, oranges, and other bright colors peppering the expansive dining room.

Jose Garces, an Iron Chef winner and celebrity chef, hails from Philadelphia but enlisted help from the Sage Restaurant Group and former Blackstone executive chef Michael Fiorello to oversee his Windy City concept. Set on the second floor of the historic Blackstone Hotel at the south end of Michigan Avenue at Millennium Park, Mercat a la Planxa is visible through floor-to-ceiling windows at the east end of the space.

"I try to focus on two types of regional cuisine, found in the coastal parts of Barcelona and up in the mountains," Fiorello said of his style when at Mercat. His style of cooking *Mar i muntanaya,* meaning the sea and the mountain in a cuisine that also draws on French, Portuguese, and Italian influences, has shaped the menu that still remains. Menu divisions include meats and seafood items cooked a la planxa (Catalan) or a la plancha (Spanish), meaning seared and caramelized on a flat cast-iron grill, as well as butternut squash dumplings with lamb and bacon, wagyu beef short ribs, and smaller, tapas-size eats such as traditional patates braves shaped into sushi-like rolls and dusted with Spanish smoked paprika.

Here Fiorello's lamb chop dish reflects a very mountain-range origin with goat cheese, chiles, and earthy mushrooms and spices.

Colorado Lamb Chops with Royal Trumpet and Porcini Mushroom Escabeche

(Serves 4)

For the lamb chops and chile rub:

½ cup minced dried ñora chiles, or other mild red chile such as ancho
½ cup water
2 plum tomatoes, seeded and diced
1 whole garlic head, roasted*
¼ cup honey

2 tablespoons chopped fresh thyme
2 tablespoons chopped fresh rosemary
1 teaspoon kosher salt
1 tablespoon freshly ground black pepper
½ cup extra-virgin olive oil
1 Colorado rack of lamb, fat cap removed, cut into 8 chops

For the mushroom escabeche:

¼ cup extra-virgin olive oil, plus 2 tablespoons
   for sautéing
¼ cup white wine vinegar
¼ cup honey
2 shallots, peeled and minced
2 roasted garlic cloves*
1 tablespoon chopped fresh thyme
1 tablespoon chopped flat-leaf parsley
1 tablespoon kosher salt
1 teaspoon freshly ground black pepper
Grated zest of 1 small lemon
4 ounces fresh royal trumpet mushrooms,
   sliced lengthwise in ⅛-inch strips
4 ounces fresh porcini mushrooms, sliced
   lengthwise in ⅛-inch strips

For the garnish:

3 ounces goat cheese, crumbled

For the chile rub, in a small skillet over medium-high heat, toast chiles until fragrant, about 2 minutes. Transfer chiles, ½ cup water, and tomatoes to a blender and puree until smooth. Squeeze roasted garlic cloves out of their skins, reserving 2 cloves for escabeche; add to the blender with honey, thyme, rosemary, salt, pepper, and olive oil and pulse to create a thick paste. Pour mixture over lamb chops in sealable plastic bags. Marinate in refrigerator for at least 2 hours, but not more than 12.

For the mushroom escabeche, whisk together ¼ cup of the oil and all ingredients except the mushrooms in a bowl and set aside. In a large sauté pan heat the remaining 2 tablespoons oil over medium-high heat. Sauté the mushrooms until they are lightly caramelized, flipping once, about 4–5 minutes. Work in batches if necessary to prevent overcrowding the pan. Add mushrooms to the vinegar mixture and chill immediately.

Heat grill to high heat. When grill is HOT, add the lamb chops, being sure to space the chops an inch apart so they cook evenly. Cook on each side for about 3 minutes for medium-rare doneness.

To serve, scoop 2 tablespoons of the mushroom escabeche, tilting the spoon to drain off some of the liquid, and place in the center of each of four plates. Place 2 lamb chops on each plate to form a circle around the mushrooms. Garnish with goat cheese.

Note: Roast garlic in a 375°F oven for 30–45 minutes or until soft. Alternatively, in a toaster oven or oven, broil the unpeeled garlic cloves until skin is blackened on both sides, about 7 minutes. Squeeze garlic from skin when cool enough to handle.

Hopleaf

5148 North Clark Street, Andersonville
(773) 334-9851
www.hopleaf.com
Owners: Michael and Louise Roper
Executive Chef: Ben Sheagren

When Michael Roper took his first bite of the smoky-cured, pink-colored stack of tender brisket sandwiched between two slices of dark rye bread during a trip to Montreal, he knew he wanted to bring the classic combo back to his restaurant in the states. Hopleaf, the Far-North-Side Andersonville institution for craft beer and bistro-inspired comfort food, has been called one of the first "gastropubs" in Chicago and the country.

Modern-day gastropubs play off the traditional British drinking spots, but with a much greater emphasis on food in the form of chef-driven menus. Hopleaf, named after the main ingredient in many of its brews, also draws heavily upon Belgian beer garden influences with both Trappist-monk-made beers and brothy mussels. On weeknights and weekends a crowd regularly packs the all-wood-clad bar downstairs, where beer connoisseurs choose from forty-plus beers on draft and more than 250 in bottles from the Midwest and around the globe. In fact, Hopleaf was one of the first Chicago bars to showcase local beers, including Goose Island, Three Floyds, Two Brothers, Bell's, Great Lakes, and Flossmoor Station.

Upstairs in the trilevel space, groups of diners celebrate loudly over shared dishes and plenty of pints in very English pub style.

An unusual favorite is the vegetarian-friendly grown-up CB&J—house-made cashew butter, fig jam, and melted Morbier cheese, perfect for the large hipster contingent known for their brew expertise. Here, though, Roper shares the meaty recipe he developed from

his many travels to Montreal. The Canadian specialty, made famous at Schwartz's Deli and known in Montreal simply as "smoked meat," differs from U.S. pastrami in that it's typically herbier, spicier, juicier, and meatier. Roper's version uses certified organic beef with a spicy rub of coriander, fennel, and cumin. He serves it stacked high on pumpernickel, but just about any artisan-quality bread will do. To achieve the traditional pink coloring found in the brisket abroad, use Insta Cure No. 1, a curing salt mixture containing sodium nitrite that is also commonly used for corned beef and is available online or in select grocery stores and gourmet retail outlets nationwide.

MONTREAL-STYLE SMOKED BRISKET SANDWICH
(Serves 8–10)

For the rub:

2 tablespoons whole black peppercorns
½ tablespoon coriander seeds
½ tablespoon cumin seeds
¾ tablespoon fennel seeds
½ tablespoon mustard seeds
1½ tablespoons celery seeds
3 allspice berries
½ tablespoon mustard powder
2 tablespoons smoked paprika
2½ tablespoons light brown sugar
2½ tablespoons kosher salt
2 tablespoons minced garlic
½ teaspoon Insta Cure No. 1 (salt and sodium nitrite) (optional)

For the brisket:

1 5-pound beef brisket
¼–½ pound thick-cut smoked bacon, cut into 6–8 strips
1 cup red wine
¾ cup hickory chips (optional)

Preheat oven to 350°F. On a baking sheet arrange peppercorns, coriander, cumin, fennel, mustard seed, celery seed, and allspice berries in a single layer. Toast in the oven for roughly 15–20 minutes, until fragrant and lightly browned. (Alternatively, toast seeds in a large sauté pan, dry, over medium-high heat, stirring often.) Allow to cool to room temperature, then transfer spices to a coffee grinder and grind to a coarse consistency.

In a small bowl, combine the ground spices with the mustard powder, paprika, brown sugar, and salt. Include the Insta Cure No. 1 if a pink meat color is desired.

Rub brisket with the garlic and then with the spice-sugar mixture, working with an aggressive massaging action. Refrigerate meat at least 1–2 hours, up to 48 hours, to allow rub to "marinate" the beef.

Preheat oven or outdoor smoker or grill to 250°F. Place brisket on a roasting pan with a rack. Layer 6–8 slices of thick cut smoked bacon along the top of the brisket. Add more bacon to completely cover the brisket if not using a smoking process. Pour the red wine in the bottom of pan and slide onto the middle rack of the oven. If you have a smoker option, place enough wet hickory chips in the smoking tray to provide 45 minutes to 1 hour of smoke (approximately 1½ cups), or set the timer on the smoking implement, if available.

Roast or smoke brisket 5 hours, basting with its own juices collected in the pan about 3–4 times during the course of the final three hours of

cooking. The brisket will be done when the meat pulls apart with gentle pressure along the grain (about 180°F internal temperature).

Allow meat to rest, covered and at room temperature, for half an hour before hand-slicing very thin. Serve with grainy mustard and rye bread or other bread of your choice.

It started in Chicago with one truck serving naan sandwiches, then another with meatballs. Cupcakes were next, then came empanadas, mac and cheese, crab cakes, short rib sandwiches, tamales, jerked chicken, and more. All served with a friendly smile from a truck.

These meals-on-wheels are a far cry from the "roach coaches" of L.A., known for their portable, tasty tacos but also, more infamously, for skirting the health department and for less-clean-than-average insides.

Acclaimed chefs around the country, from celebrity cooks to the fine-dining trained, have now joined the fleet of food trucks rolling across the nation, from Los Angeles, San Francisco, and Seattle to New York City and Atlanta. In Portland and Austin, clusters of parked food trailers have formed mini open-air markets, filled with street food goodness galore.

It all started around 2008, when economic recession hit hard. Really hard. Many restaurants closed. Thousands of chefs, cooks, and waitstaff were out of work. The everyday consumer had stopped dining out and started eating in.

Chicago chefs jumped on the bandwagon as much as they could. When former mayor Richard M. Daley declared that hot dog carts and other similar mobile or street-based operations posed a health hazard, the decision had been made. No food can be prepared on a truck or cart and then sold and served to the public. Period.

But that doesn't mean food can't be prepared off-site, in a commercial kitchen, and sold off a truck already cooked. So, when the trend rolled into the Windy City, a couple of veteran chefs bucked the bricks-and-mortar boundaries, taking their food to the streets and their voices to City Hall.

The point man was experienced chef Matt Maroni, owner of Gaztro-Wagon and the proclaimed founder of the mobile food truck movement in Chicago, who wanted to open a truck but came up against the prohibiting laws. Theoretically, Chicago should have the same rights as other food-truck-friendly cities, being a place legendary for its street food, from cheesy pizza and all-beef hot dogs to overstuffed burritos, traveling tamales, Italian beef sandwiches, pierogis, and more. To Maroni and many other chefs and restaurateurs who would follow in his footsteps, this next step toward mobile food trucks only made sense.

"Chicago is such a great culinary city—there are plenty of people with great ideas and great concepts, and food trucks add another avenue for people to be creative," Maroni says. "People are chomping at the bit for this— they see the trucks in New York and L.A. and wonder why Chicago doesn't have them."

After some due diligence researching municipal codes and permit procedures, Maroni drafted an ordinance that would make room for the trucks, sharing the proposal with friends who work for his local chamber of commerce. They in turn took the proposal to local alderman Scott Waguespack, who took an interest in the issue and worked with legislative committees to review the proposal, where it still remains.

"Once I saw there wasn't an ordinance for us, I could have stomped my feet and thrown my hands up, but I decided to put a pen to paper instead," Maroni says. He also put himself to work—opening a storefront with a small

commercial kitchen that could prepare food for the truck as well as sell on-site. For lunch and dinner Maroni combines the chef-driven art of cooking that is "gastronomy" with the portable affordability of street food for a menu of naan-bread-based sandwiches stuffed with creative pairings like braised lamb with creamed mushrooms and English pea pesto, pork pozole with hominy, lobster with potato leek hash and brie cheese, or roast venison with acorn squash, date jam, and hazelnuts.

After Maroni came Philip Foss, the fine-dining-trained executive chef of three-star Lockwood (page 26) in the historic Palmer House Hotel, who started his truck, The Meatyballs Mobile, and came to Maroni's side to advocate for a revision of the laws. Originally contemplating a doughnut shop, Foss switched to the more savory meatballs idea after cooking them at home one night and thinking it would make for an even better casual restaurant concept. When Foss realized he could sell them off a truck, that made it even better. Except when he ran into the strict laws.

To work around those limitations, Foss and his wife Kenni rented a licensed commercial kitchen space where they start cooking at 8 a.m. They get the sandwiches, wrapped and hot, on the truck by 10:30 or 11 a.m. for lunch, then hit the streets, "tweeting" their location in case interested patrons didn't see the schedule already posted on their website. Then it's back to the kitchen to prep for the next day.

What began as a limited menu of a few different kinds of meatballs has expanded to include a smoked pork shoulder in bourbon-cola barbecue sauce, chicken curry with chutney, seafood-based balls, and an adventurous version, to say the least: bull's testicles.

"There are three main reasons why I think food trucks are great for the city," Foss says. "Number one, it's creating more jobs. Obviously, when more businesses open up, there's more employment to be had. It also offers an inexpensive start-up option for chefs and other people who want to open up their own restaurants." Third, they simply make for more fun-filled, interactive eating.

These trucks aren't your typical roach coach of the days long ago. Today they come equipped with the latest equipment and high-tech generators powerful enough to work in the rain, sleet, snow, and cold that Chicagoans see plenty of. They're cleaned daily and run through the same city health inspections as a traditional restaurant. And, decorated like an artist's canvas, the trucks are also backed by an online identity that typically includes a just as colorful website and Twitter feed that both announces stops and chats up customers in an ongoing digital dialogue.

Now, with a somewhat rebounded economy, many chefs have kept their restaurant posts, launching these trucks as secondary outposts and outlets for creativity that double as a clever marketing and business-building campaign. It's as if they've put a face to their Twitter feeds, literally, with some wheels and good old street food in a new era of restaurant branding.

When the first trucks made their first stops in the business districts of the Loop and the River North neighborhood, ever so slowly, office workers caught wind of the street-side sights, sounds, and scrumptious smells that put their brown bag lunches of peanut butter and jelly sandwiches to shame. Now truck operators say it's hard to keep up with the core group of regulars that seem to build day by day, meal by meal, within a legal framework that prevents them from replenishing on-site.

But demand drives supply. And laws. Chicagoans have rallied behind these trucks, and for good reason. The food is tasty. It's portable. It's affordable. And it's created a community of happy, experimental eaters who can meet their beloved chefs face to face and talk with fellow food lovers both on-site and online in the most modern type of restaurant or dinner table of its kind.

THE PUBLICAN

837 WEST FULTON MARKET, FULTON MARKET
(312) 733-9555
WWW.THEPUBLICANRESTAURANT.COM
CO-OWNER–EXECUTIVE CHEF: PAUL KAHAN
CO-OWNER: DONNIE MADIA
CHEF DE CUISINE: BRIAN HOUSTON

Revered Chicago chef Paul Kahan and restaurateur Donnie Madia created their third venture, The Publican, in a testament to all things pork, emblemized by the menu of pork chops, belly, hams, ribs, and sausages, and by the life-size drawing of a pig on the main wall. So encountering chef de cuisine Brian Houston's recipe for veal sweetbreads seems unusual. Yet the swap perfectly reflects Houston's diverse cooking regimen outside swine: Aside from the sweetbreads, he's also known for garlic-infused mussels, fisherman's stew, and a lineup of raw oysters and crudos, composed salads with roasted beets, delicate greens, and other Illinois finds, lamb cassoulet, and juicy farm chicken.

Still, the three-tiered, crispy-fatty-chunky pork belly reigns at this all-wood German-style beer hall reminiscent of ones you'd see in Munich, where rowdy beer swiggers link arms in festive debauchery and song. Here it's toned down a bit, though still loud and boisterous thanks to the semi-open "booths," endless communal tables with high-backed chairs, center-of-the-room "islands" for congregating and perching, and extensive craft beer menu with handfuls of local, German, and strong Belgian brews. In fact, the space so much resembles a modern beer hall that it took home James Beard's top honor for restaurant design one year after opening. Large white fabric "orbs" for light fixtures hang from overhead, while beer taps line the counter at the open kitchen where chefs can be seen hard at work.

The Kahan-Madia team's pick of location also fits in with the meat-focused approach, tucked in the center of Chicago's Fulton Market neighborhood, also known as the

meatpacking and warehouse district where many a pork processor butchered and sold their goods. While The Publican's known mainly for pork, other dishes shine just as strong, such as the veal sweetbreads. When preparing them at home, sweetbreads can be special-ordered from most butchers or purchased online through various companies dedicated to the humane treatment of the animal.

THE PUBLICAN'S VEAL SWEETBREADS
(Serves 4)

For the court bouillon:

3 quarts cold water
2 750-ml bottles white wine
6 large yellow onions, minced
1 large carrot, sliced
1 rib celery, sliced
Large bouquet garni
½ cup salt
1 tablespoon whole black peppercorns

For the sweetbreads:

1 pound veal sweetbreads, rinsed under cold water
1 cup quick-mixing flour, such as Wondra*
4 tablespoons butter, softened
1 tablespoon palm sugar
2 tablespoons extra-virgin olive oil

Combine all ingredients for court bouillon in a large saucepan. Bring to a boil over high heat. Reduce heat, add sweetbreads, and poach at a gentle simmer for 5 minutes, stirring once.

Pour sweetbreads and court bouillon into a metal bowl set over a large bowl of ice. Cool sweetbreads, stirring occasionally. Remove sweetbreads; refrigerate court bouillon for another use. Peel off and discard outer membrane from the sweetbreads and separate into four 4-ounce portions. Dredge lightly in flour. Combine butter and palm sugar; set aside.

Sauté the sweetbreads in the oil in a medium skillet until lightly browned on both sides, basting occasionally with the palm sugar butter. Serve warm with a variety of sauces (mustard, barbecue, honey, etc.) or treat them as croutons and serve them in a salad.

__Note:__ Wondra, a flour developed for lump-free blending in sauces and gravies, has lately been used by chefs to create a lighter, airy breading for frying. If Wondra flour is unavailable, combine 1 cup all-purpose flour with 1½ teaspoons baking powder and ½ teaspoon salt. Use this mixture for the recipe.

KARYN'S

KARYN'S RAW CAFÉ
1901 NORTH HALSTED STREET, RIVER NORTH
(312) 255-1590
WWW.KARYNRAW.COM

KARYN'S COOKED
738 NORTH WELLS STREET, LINCOLN PARK
(312) 587-1050
WWW.KARYNRAW.COM

KARYN'S ON GREEN
130 SOUTH GREEN STREET, GREEKTOWN
(312) 226-6155
WWW.KARYNSONGREEN.COM
CHEF-OWNER: KARYN CALABRESE

Karyn Calabrese is in her sixties, but, looking at her, that seems like a joke. The slender, fresh-faced brunette started off as a vegetarian decades ago, but later explored raw food eating as a newly single mom looking to boost her energy. She bought her first wheatgrass juicer, and the rest was history.

Though the raw food concept seems extreme, Calabrese has developed a cult following of sorts, with many regulars still flocking to her original Karyn's Raw Café for in-house dining and takeout shopping.

Still, wanting to welcome more types of eaters, Calabrese opened her second outpost, Karyn's Cooked, the cooked-food version of her vegetarian raw restaurant that's a favorite among non–meat eaters and meat eaters alike. She also runs a holistic therapy center, Karyn's Inner Beauty Center, teaches detox classes, makes regular TV and speaking appearances, and finds just about any way she can to educate Chicagoans and eaters around the country about the benefits of holistic cuisine.

Now, as others have caught up with forward-thinking Calabrese and embraced this "cleaner" way of eating, her latest endeavor, Karyn's on Green in the Greektown neighborhood, steps up the sexiness of her philosophy with sleeker décor, a lively full-service bar (healthy drinks, of course), and more sophisticated vegetarian dishes like beet carpaccio with a salad of kale, rainbow chard, tofu feta, and champagne vinaigrette; a raw pasta made from nut meal with zucchini, beech mushrooms, and cashew basil pesto; and a wild mushroom risotto with orange-infused gin and fried rosemary. Calabrese's vegan shepherd's pie reminds us we can still eat the comfort foods we crave, but in healthier manifestations.

VEGAN SHEPHERD'S PIE

(Serves 2)

For the stew:

4 ounces crumbled Italian-sausage-style seitan
½ cup diced carrots
½ cup diced parsnips
¼ cup diced celery
¼ cup diced red onion
1 teaspoon minced garlic
1 tablespoon tomato paste
¼ teaspoon fresh thyme
¼ teaspoon fresh oregano
Salt and freshly ground black pepper, to taste
Water, as needed

For the potatoes:

2 small Yukon Gold potatoes, peeled
1 tablespoon chives
2 teaspoons grated and minced horseradish
Salt and freshly ground black pepper, to taste

For the red wine gravy:

1 tablespoon olive oil
1 tablespoon flour
1 cup red wine
1 teaspoon minced fresh rosemary
Pinch of salt
Water, as needed

In a large sauté pan or saucepan over medium-high heat, combine the seitan, carrots, parsnips, celery, onion, and garlic and sauté until onion is tender and translucent. Add the tomato paste, thyme, and oregano, seasoning with salt and pepper. Add just enough water to thin the mixture slightly. Lower heat and simmer covered until vegetables are tender, about 30 minutes.

Boil potatoes in a medium-size pot over high heat until cooked through and tender, about 10 minutes. Drain potatoes and mash in the pot or a mixing bowl. Add chives, horseradish, salt, and pepper, adjusting seasonings.

Preheat the broiler. To make the gravy, in a sauté pan over medium heat, whisk together the oil and flour until smooth. Add the red wine and rosemary, stirring frequently. Season with salt and add water as needed to thin to a gravy consistency, stirring frequently. Remove gravy from heat but keep warm.

Divide stew evenly between two bowls. Add the gravy and spread mashed potatoes on top. Place under the broiler for about 2 minutes, or until potato topping is golden and slightly crispy along the edges.

PORK

Once declared the largest hog producer in the nation, Illinois now falls far short of Iowa, but lately the growing output of smaller, noncommercial, family pork-producing farms has fueled a trend in the city toward consumption of artisanal, locally and sustainably raised pork (meaning pork raised outside on pasture and not in confinement operations). In fact, in the last few years, a handful of chefs and restaurateurs have opened up new places dedicated to all things pork, from Paul Kahan's Publican to Jimmy Bannos and Scott Harris's Purple Pig, and to a wave of chefs learning to butcher their own whole hogs in their kitchens.

One of them, Rob Levitt, has since left his popular restaurant Mado to open his own butcher shop dedicated to pork and other artisanal, sustainably produced meats, occasionally hosting pig-butchering demonstrations. Paul Kahan has announced plans for a butcher shop as well. Chris Pandel at The Bristol has teamed up with other chefs to help them and others learn the carving art. And for one whole day, there's Baconfest, a celebration of bacon and bacon-laced foods, bacon crafts, bacon spirits, and more, with an extensive roster of sponsoring restaurants and chefs.

Until the last decade or so, it was a challenge for the everyday consumer to access not only high-quality bacon but also the thick, fatty, juicy cuts of Berkshire pork typically available only to high-end restaurants. Now there's thick and buttery seared pork belly, tender pork loin, pulled barbecued pork, babyback pork ribs, braised pork shoulder, pork tacos and carnitas, pork sausage, pork-based charcuterie—even crispy pork skins and pig's feet have made an appearance on local menus. That includes whole roasted pig's face at Stephanie Izard's Girl & the Goat.

While the trend has slowed a bit, pork is still a much sought-after food, certainly a testament to Chicago's hearty, meat-heavy Midwestern culture.

THE PURPLE PIG

500 NORTH MICHIGAN AVENUE, MAG MILE
(312) 464-1744
WWW.THEPURPLEPIGCHICAGO.COM
OWNERS-PROPRIETORS: JIMMY BANNOS, SCOTT HARRIS, AND
    TONY MANTUANO
EXECUTIVE CHEF: JIMMY BANNOS JR.

The name Jimmy Bannos in Chicago brings up a few images: chunky andouille sausage gumbo, red beans and rice, shrimp and grits. Heaven on Seven, the original location on Wabash Avenue (Jewelers Row), has for decades fed hungry Chicagoans the soul food and hot sauce varieties straight out of New Orleans. Now, Bannos says, he's lucky his son has decided to follow in the family footsteps, and so we have The Purple Pig, a fun and lively eatery focused on pork and wine (the pig is purple from too much red wine) with a collection of small plates for sharing and sampling.

The menu also includes a strong selection of Midwestern and artisanal cheeses, cured meats and other house-made charcuterie, delicate seafood dishes like olive-oil-poached tuna with Greek lima beans, and Laughing Bird shrimp and clams, as well as seasonal Midwestern vegetable creations, from brussels sprouts, artichokes, and beets in the fall to tender greens in the spring.

"We're focusing on nose-to-tail cooking, as they call it," says Jimmy Bannos Jr., executive chef. "We're trying lots of different stuff, like pig's ears, liver, and tail but we keep it all

approachable and simple." Bannos has accomplished the impossible: making pig's ears one of the best-selling dishes on the menu. The pork neck-bone rillette with hot mustard also holds its own.

"Pork is important to so many cuisines, from Italy to Spain and other Mediterranean cuisines," Bannos says. "We didn't want to go overboard with it either, so we've tried to think of dishes so there is something for everybody." Here's a simple but elegant dish for both die-hard pork lovers and the occasional pork eater. Milk together with other liquids helps tenderize the meat by adding a touch of creaminess without extra acid.

MILK-BRAISED PORK SHOULDER AND CREAMY MASHED POTATOES
(Serves 8)

For the pork:

3–4 pounds pork shoulder, bone removed, cut into
   8-ounce pieces
Salt and freshly ground black pepper, to taste
2 tablespoons canola or grapeseed oil
4 onions, peeled and quartered
4 large carrots, peeled and cut into large pieces
2 celery ribs, cut into 6 pieces
1 small bunch fresh thyme
5 bay leaves
2 gallons milk
2 gallons pork stock, chicken stock, or low-sodium
   chicken broth

For the potatoes:

1¼ pounds russet potatoes, peeled and
   cut into 1½-inch chunks
¼ cup heavy cream
4 teaspoons butter
½ teaspoon salt
¼ teaspoon freshly ground black pepper

Preheat oven to 350°F.

Season pork with salt and pepper. Wrap a piece of string around each pork piece from one end to the other, securing tightly like a small roast.

In a large roasting pan over medium-high heat, using two burners, heat oil and sear pork to create a caramelized crust and hold in juices, about 2–3 minutes per side. Add vegetables, herbs, milk, and stock and bring to a boil.

Slide roasting pan into the oven and roast until pork and vegetables are tender, about 2–3 hours.

Meanwhile, prepare the mashed potatoes. Cover potatoes in a large stockpot with salted water. Bring to a boil and cook until tender, about 15–20 minutes. While they are cooking, warm the cream. Drain potatoes and return to the pot. Mash using a potato masher or wooden spoon, add cream, butter, salt, and pepper, and continue mashing until well mixed. Set aside.

Drain pork and vegetables, reserving 2 cups of the liquid. Chop vegetables into small pieces and set aside. Remove string from pork and slice against the grain into 2-inch-thick slices.

In a small saucepan, reduce liquid to about half or until it thickens slightly. Scoop mashed potatoes onto eight plates, top with vegetables and pork slices, and drizzle with sauce.

BIG STAR

1531 NORTH DAMEN AVENUE, WICKER PARK
(773) 680-7740
WWW.BIGSTARCHICAGO.COM
CO-OWNER–EXECUTIVE CHEF: PAUL KAHAN
CO-OWNER: DONNIE MADIA
CHEF DE CUISINE: JUSTIN LARGE

Tacos and whiskey. In their fourth venture, directly across the street from the already successful Violet Hour (see page 100, Chicago's Cocktail Culture), Donnie Madia and Paul Kahan have zeroed in on the city's street food culture and its affinity for Mexican-American foods, strong drinks, and spirited spaces. Formerly Pontiac Café, known for its dive-y feel and boisterous indoor/outdoor gatherings, Big Star plays off this culture with a central wraparound bar surrounded by booths drawing youthful crowds inside, while a walk-up window for to-go orders gives on a big open-air patio during the warmer months.

Manning the kitchen is Justin Large, who can be seen from time to time through a small window off to the side of the space. Tacos are cheap, tasty, and varied, from braised pork belly tacos with tomato-guajillo sauce in a homemade soft corn tortilla, to the wood-grilled chicken thigh tacos with chorizo, to the veggie-only tacos de rajas de poblano (roasted peppers and salty queso blanco cheese with smooth crema).

Tacos al pastor (shepherd style) developed in Mexico when Lebanese immigrants introduced the locals to shawarma, or spit-grilled meat, usually made with lamb. In Mexico, where lamb is scarcer, the tacos are typically made with pork. The pork is marinated

overnight or for two days in a liquid chile mixture, rubbed with spices, and then roasted on a spit or vertical rotisserie, much like Greek gyros. Basting with acidic pineapple juice helps tenderize and caramelize the meat even further.

At Big Star, Large and his team cook their tacos al pastor in this authentic way, using a large vertical rotisserie from which they can shave off thin slices of the pork. Most home cooks, however, don't own a spit-roaster. Create a similar effect by setting a traditional oven at a low temperature and slow-roasting the pork, turning and basting frequently with the pineapple juice.

Tacos al Pastor ("Spit-Roasted" Pork Tacos)
(Serves 6–12)

For the marinade:

2 ounces guajillo chiles
½ ounce ancho chiles
½ tablespoon canned chipotle chiles,
    drained and finely chopped
¼ cup orange juice
Dash of cocktail bitters
2 ounces Coca-Cola
¼ cup plus 2 tablespoons apple cider vinegar
1 tablespoon light brown sugar
½ clove garlic, minced

For the spice rub:

1½ teaspoons annatto seed
¾ teaspoon dried oregano
¼ teaspoon cumin seed
¼ teaspoon ground cinnamon
2 whole cloves
½ teaspoon whole black peppercorns
1 teaspoon salt
1 teaspoon brown sugar
2 whole garlic cloves

For the pork:

2 pounds boneless pork shoulder or
    pork butt roast
2 small yellow onions, quartered
¼ fresh pineapple, cut into thick slices
½ dried chile de arbol pepper, minced
½ cup pineapple juice

For serving:

Corn tortillas
1 small red onion, diced
1 bunch cilantro, chopped

For the marinade, stem and seed chiles, breaking each into small pieces. Soak the chiles in boiling water for 30 minutes. Drain the chiles and place in a blender. Add orange juice, bitters, Coca-Cola, and vinegar and pulse until smooth. Add the sugar and garlic and blend an additional 30 seconds. Pour marinade over pork in a large plastic resealable bag or large bowl. Close bag or cover bowl. Refrigerate pork at least 6–8 hours or overnight, but no more than 36 hours, turning pork over once.

Preheat oven to 350°F. Discard marinade and lightly pat pork dry with paper towels. Grind the annatto seed, oregano, cumin, cinnamon, cloves, and peppercorns together in a grinder or crush using a mortar and pestle. Combine spices with the salt, sugar, and garlic and rub spice mixture on all sides of pork.

Place pork in a shallow roasting pan with the onion. Line pineapple slices along the top of the pork. Make a basting sauce by stirring the chile de arbol into the pineapple juice. Bake 3 hours or until pork is very tender, basting the pork with the juice mixture several times.

Remove pork from oven and let rest 10 minutes. Thinly slice pork or use two forks to pull the pork into shreds. Serve with the roasted onion and pineapple on warmed corn tortillas garnished with the red onion and cilantro.

The Bristol

2152 North Damen Avenue, Bucktown
(773) 862-5555
www.thebristolchicago.com
Owners: John Ross and Phillip Walters
Executive Chef: Chris Pandel

Chris Pandel isn't afraid of a little offal. In fact, he loves the often-discarded animal parts. The fine-dining-trained chef was also one of the first wave of chefs to start experimenting with whole-animal butchering. Cases in point: stewed tripe with chickpeas and seared beef heart with artichoke, spinach, and creamy béarnaise.

His chicken liver mousse is something of a novelty—in fact, since he reintroduced the old-school delicacy, serving it as a scoopable, airy butter in white espresso cups with a little extra cream and whipping, it's been a much re-created dish on other restaurant menus in town. He may have started the trend for roast bone marrow as butter, too. Copycats? Maybe. Flattering replication? Definitely.

Pandel has a special affinity for pork, carving up the meat at the back of the house for various uses, including charcuterie and bacon, roast tenderloin, braised shoulder, and a sausage stuffing for Scotch olives. But he also makes his own silky pastas, perhaps pairing braised boar with pappardelle, serving simple ricotta ravioli with browned butter, or mixing other hand-cut noodles with chiles and Parmesan.

Both The Bristol and its followers describe it as a very "neighborhood" restaurant, an approachable space with plenty of woods and warm colors, and a nice-sized front bar where mixologists change up the menu for cocktails as often as Pandel does for the kitchen. It's the quintessential modern Midwestern meal—comfort food relics with contemporary spins, earthy meats and seasonal vegetables with perfectly paired wines, craft beers, and cocktails. Pandel draws on his other affinity for Italian cuisine with this pork-based spin on the classic vitello tonnato, a creamy tuna sauce normally served with cold sliced veal.

Bacon-Wrapped Pork Loin Tonnato

(Serves 6–8)

For the pork and brine:

2 cups kosher salt
1 tablespoon curing salt, optional
1 cup sugar
4 quarts water
2 cloves garlic, minced
10 whole black peppercorns
5 sprigs fresh rosemary
10 parsley stems
1 bay leaf
1 boneless pork loin, about 4½ pounds
12–14 slices (about 1 pound) thick-cut bacon

For the garlic aioli:

4 egg yolks
1 clove fresh garlic, finely grated
Dash of white or rice vinegar
Pinch of salt
2 cups vegetable oil

For the tonnato sauce:

1 3-ounce can Albacore tuna packed in oil, drained
3 tablespoons minced capers
3 tablespoons minced red onion
½ teaspoon minced fresh marjoram
¼ cup thinly sliced fresh parsley leaves
1 tablespoon red wine vinegar
1 oil-packed anchovy fillet, mashed
Juice of ½ lemon
¼ teaspoon kosher salt
¼ teaspoon freshly ground black pepper

For the salad:

6 tablespoons extra-virgin olive oil
2 tablespoons freshly squeezed lemon juice
Pinch of kosher salt and freshly ground black pepper

2 bunches fresh arugula (about ½ pound)
2 tablespoons (½ ounce) shaved pecorino Romano cheese

For the brine, in a large bowl, stir together salt, curing salt (if desired) sugar, and water until dissolved. Add garlic, peppercorns, and herbs and pour over pork loin in a deep roasting pan or Cambro cooler. Brine pork in refrigerator for at least 4 hours or up to three days before roasting.

Preheat oven to 300°F.

Discard brine and pat pork loin dry. Wrap the bacon slices around the pork loin to cover completely, tying with string to secure. Roast pork until internal temperature reads 145°F, checking after 30 minutes. When done, let rest 10 minutes. Refrigerate at least 1 hour or overnight.

Next, prepare the garlic aioli. In a food processor or blender, place the yolks, garlic, vinegar, and salt, pulsing a few times to combine. Blending at moderate speed, slowly pour in the vegetable oil until mixture becomes thick and creamy. Alternatively, whisk together the first four ingredients by hand in a large bowl and slowly pour in the oil, whisking constantly.

To prepare the tonnato sauce, add the tuna to the aioli in the food processor or blender, and process until smooth. If mixing by hand, mash tuna thoroughly before incorporating into aioli. Scrape tuna mixture into a bowl. Fold in remaining ingredients and adjust seasonings as necessary.

To serve, slice pork loin into thin pieces and arrange on six or eight plates. Drizzle tonnato sauce evenly over pork. Whisk together oil, lemon juice, salt, and pepper and toss with arugula to coat. Arrange salad evenly atop pork. Garnish with pecorino shavings.

URBAN BELLY / BELLY SHACK

URBAN BELLY
3053 NORTH CALIFORNIA AVENUE, AVONDALE
(773) 583-0500
WWW.URBANBELLYCHICAGO.COM

BELLY SHACK
1912 NORTH WESTERN AVENUE, WICKER PARK
(773) 252-1414
WWW.BELLYSHACK.COM
CHEF-OWNER: BILL KIM

Le Lan, during its half decade in existence, was a destination for fine-dining French-Asian cooking as well as a breeding ground for many great chefs in the city. That group included Roland Liccioni, the former head of Les Nomades, Arun Sampanthavivat of Arun's, the city's only fine-dining Thai restaurant, and Bill Kim, proclaimed a rising star during that time.

Since Le Lan closed, Kim continues to rise and shine, using the fine-dining techniques he refined there and while working for Charlie Trotter and Shawn McClain, in his anything-but-fine-dining restaurants, both of which exploded with popularity the minute they opened (first Urban Belly, and a couple years later, Belly Shack). Born in Korea but raised mostly in America, Kim sought to bring the comfort food he enjoyed growing up to the masses here, from crispy rice and super-soft dumplings to his trademark brothy noodles, homemade kimchi, and pork belly.

"I always dreamed of opening up a noodle shop, ever since I was eighteen," he says. "But the more I worked in fine dining, the more I got away from that childhood memory. It was when I was working in Philadelphia that I thought more about Asian food and realized I could really do this instead of just as a hobby."

While Urban Belly is the incarnation of that dream in a blend of different Asian foods and dishes, Belly Shack combines Korean food with Latin American flavors in honor of his wife, Yvonne, who has a Puerto Rican and Spanish background.

"Going to my mother-in-law's house opened me up further to Latin cuisine and Puerto Rican food," Kim says. "I had never tasted anything like tostones, and she really encouraged me to open up Belly Shack." The fried plantain chips make an appearance, loaded with chimichurri for tostones and also in bigger, thicker form as enclosures for a Puerto Rican–Chicago jibarito, here stuffed with Chinese black beans and marinated tofu instead of the traditional spiced steak, lettuce, and tomato.

Rather than simply calling this style of cooking "fusion," Kim instead focuses on using the best ingredients possible (that means sliced jicama if fresh water chesnuts can't be found), combined with classic culinary techniques in a very fine-dining approach, even if his restaurants veer far from that end of the spectrum in service and décor. Casual, affordable, and BYOB, both places use counter service, with waitstaff in the rustic dining room only for drink refills and dish clearing. Tunes from indie bands and the Buena Vista Social Club soundtrack piped in the background and urban-abstract artwork, both in-house and online, help create a youthful, funky vibe. His recipe here represents that perfect blend of brothy Korean stews, pork, and kimchi with hominy, cilantro, and cumin, commonly used in Mexico and South and Central America.

KIMCHI STEW WITH BRAISED PORK BELLY
(Serves 6)

For the pork:

1 cup fish sauce
½ cup sweet chile sauce
½ cup brown sugar
½ cup mirin
½ cup Sriracha
½ cup Korean chile paste
4 pounds of pork belly or pork butt, cut in pieces
   to fit in roasting pan

For the broth:

6 cups unsalted or low-sodium chicken stock or
   broth
2½ cups sweet chile sauce
1 cup soy sauce
1 cup fish sauce
½ cup Korean chile paste
2 pounds flat, oval Korean rice cakes
2 cups chopped napa kimchi
1 12-ounce can hominy, rinsed
Juice of 2 limes

For the garnish:

2 tablespoons toasted cumin seeds
¼ cup chopped cilantro
¼ cup chopped garlic chives

Preheat the oven to 300°F. Combine the fish sauce, sweet chile sauce, brown sugar, mirin, Sriracha, and chile paste in a large bowl. Pour mixture over the pork until almost completely covered.

Roast pork in the oven for about 2 hours, turning after 1 hour. The pork should be tender and cooked through. Remove from oven. When cool enough to handle, cut pork into 1-inch chunks and set aside.

Heat chicken broth in a large pot over medium-high heat. Add the sweet chile sauce, soy sauce, fish sauce, and Korean chile paste and simmer for 5 minutes. Add the pork, rice cakes, napa kimchi, and hominy and continue to simmer until rice cakes are tender, about 5 more minutes.

Add lime juice and ladle stew evenly into 6 bowls. Garnish with toasted cumin, chopped cilantro, and garlic chives.

Don Juan Restaurante / Patricio

6730 North Northwest Highway, Edison Park
(773) 775-6438
Owner: Maria Concannon

Maria Concannon has seen her share of challenges—emigrating from Mexico, learning English, starting up her own business, raising three children as a single mom, dealing with a restaurant fire, and more. Despite it all, Concannon shines. Forever smiling, forever joking, forever hospitable, Concannon is the light of her restaurant and everyone she touches.

You can taste this happiness, this love of people and of life, in her food. After almost thirty years in business, it's not always so easy to continue feeding that passion as well as others without getting burned out. Beyond the restaurant doors, Concannon also continues to educate and inspire others about Mexican cooking, and she has remained an active member of Les Dames d'Escoffier, a prestigious association of women in culinary society. Inside, she's constantly roaming the dining room to chat with friends, regulars, and newcomers alike, beaming as usual.

Tucked on a little side street off the main drag in Edison Park, a quiet, family-friendly, blue-collar neighborhood on the Northwest Side, Don Juan stands slightly hidden, noticeable mainly by its yellow lit sign and friendly valet parker.

With arched stucco walls and a brown-tiled floor, wooden tables, and curvy wrought-iron chairs, Don Juan resembles a traditional casual cantina, but it's not your typical Americanized burrito joint. Concannon's place is known more for its authentic regional Mexican dishes, from Mexico City–style tacos with a few simple ingredients on homemade tortillas, to seafood nachos and fresh fish characteristic of Puerto Vallarta and the coastline, to steaks and chops from the heart of the country.

Concannon takes her guacamole as seriously as she took child raising, sourcing only the best buttery Mexican Haas avocados she can find and mixing in the diced onions and cilantro at the very last minute before it hits the table "so it stays fresh," she says. Then there are Concannon's enchiladas with her famous mole she takes days to make with twelve different types of chile peppers, toasted seeds, breadcrumbs, and a touch of chocolate all simmered and melded together.

On the right side of Don Juan's through a separate entryway is Patricio, the more intimate white-tablecloth sibling started up in 1990 by her son Patrick, who cooked in the kitchens of France and later trained under Charlie Trotter. For ten years Patrick ran Patricio, developing the menu and a name for himself as a master of blending the French techniques and creativity he honed under Trotter with Mexican traditions to put his own stamp on fine dining. One example is his pork tenderloin in pasilla sauce—tenderly roasted pork with a traditional chile-tomatillo sauce common in Oaxaca.

MEDALLONES DE PUERCO EN CHILE PASILLA (PORK TENDERLOIN IN PASILLA SAUCE)
(Serves 6)

6 to 8 pasilla chile peppers, halved and seeded
1 pound tomatillos, husked and diced
½ onion, diced
3 garlic cloves, minced
Salt and freshly ground black pepper, to taste
2 1-pound pork tenderloins
2½ tablespoons corn oil, divided
Corn tortillas

Combine pasilla chiles, tomatillos, onion, and garlic in a saucepan and add water to cover. Bring to a boil over high heat. Reduce heat and simmer, uncovered, 5 minutes or until vegetables are softened. Drain vegetables, reserving half of the liquid. In a blender, puree the vegetables with a touch of the reserved liquid until very smooth, about 1–2 minutes.

In a skillet over medium heat, cook pureed vegetables in 1 tablespoon of the corn oil until liquid evaporates and sauce is thick enough to coat the back of a spoon. Add more reserved liquid if sauce gets too thick. Season with salt.

Preheat the oven to 350°F. Season pork tenderloins with salt and pepper. In an ovenproof skillet over medium-high heat, heat the remaining 1½ tablespoon of corn oil and cook pork until a crust forms on both sides, about 2 minutes per side. Transfer skillet to the oven and roast until internal temperature reaches 145–150°F. Remove from the oven and let rest 10 minutes before slicing pork into 1½–2-inch slices

To serve, divide slices evenly among six plates, spooning the warm pasilla sauce over the pork. Serve with warmed corn tortillas.

ASIANS IN CHICAGO

The Chicago neighborhood map looks like a quilt on paper. And those patchworks were sewn together years ago, when immigrant groups came to the city and naturally segregated themselves in the 1920s through the 1950s to support each other with employment, language help, and general immersion assistance.

That patchwork pattern can still be seen today, and that includes various Asian communities. Chinatown, the largest of such communities, located on the South Side toward Twenty-Second Street and Wentworth Avenue just east of the once Italian-heavy Bridgeport neighborhood, took shape as far back as the late 1800s and early 1900s, when many Chinese immigrants came to Chicago to help dig the Chicago Sanitary and Ship Canal, once a portal for goods transport that's now used for carrying treated sewage into Lake Michigan.

The first wave of Chinese restaurants also occurred around this time, and many of the openings were linked to politics, according to research from the Chinese-American Museum of Chicago. In 1905, politically controversial alderman Hinky Dink Kenna leased space to Chin Foin's King Yen Lo Restaurant, and in 1907 the Empire Reform Association opened King Joy Lo, later managed by Foin, as a way to raise funds to support political activities back in China.

Many of the finer Chinese restaurants closed during the Great Depression and were replaced by more affordable eateries. Today that pattern continues, save for fine-dining institution Shanghai Terrace at the Peninsula Hotel, but these restaurants run the gamut in style and cuisine, from Szechuan to Cantonese and dim sum, Peking barbecue, Mongolian barbecue, and the more Americanized chop suey.

A handful of Chinese restaurants are also scattered further north in the Uptown neighborhood near Argyle and Broadway Streets in an area known more as Little Vietnam. According to the Chicago History Museum's *Encyclopedia of Chicago,* Vietnamese immigrants came to Chicago in droves during the late 1970s, many as refugees from the Vietnam War and the fall of Saigon. Peppered with storefront eateries serving French-Vietnamese baked goods or big bowls of brothy noodle soups called pho, this community is as popular for eating among the Asians who live there as it is among residents from across the city. Downtown, Le Colonial (page 150) remains an institution for fine French-Vietnamese cuisine, once rivaled by the former Le Lan, where Korean-born Bill Kim (Urban Belly, page 126) rose to fame.

But the lines get blurry around Uptown and further west in the Albany Park neighborhood on the Northwest Side where many Korean, Thai, and Filipino influences can be seen throughout both neighborhoods and everywhere in between. And the melting pot of food shows it, from the crackling rice and sunny-side-up eggs of Korean bibimbap, to peanut-y pad thai and caramelized pad see ew, to yellow and green curries infused with coconut milk, spices, and chiles.

Albany Park is also home to many residents of Thai descent. Thai-born Arun Sampanthavivat of Arun's (page 131) has worked to rebuild the Thai Community Center at the heart of the community. An unofficial Koreatown takes shape near there in the area bounded by Pulaski, Montrose, Foster, and Clark, although Koreans have been living and working in many parts of Chicago since the 1920s. Japanese influences in Chicago's culinary scene are so prevalent throughout restaurants small and big, casual and fine, the cuisine is considered mainstream by many.

Regardless of quilts and patchwork, these days, though the neighborhood maps may look similar to those from the 1940s and 1950s, the actual living and breathing communities are a hodgepodge of Asian backgrounds, histories, cultures, foods, flavors, and tastes that all Chicagoans and visitors can enjoy.

ARUN'S

4156 NORTH KEDZIE AVENUE, IRVING PARK
(773) 539-1909
WWW.ARUNSTHAI.COM
CHEF-OWNER: ARUN SAMPANTHAVIVAT

Where Joho has fine-dining French, Mantuano has fine-dining Italian, Bayless has fine-dining Mexican, and Trotter has fine-dining American, Arun Sampanthavivat has fine-dining Thai. Since 1985, the restaurant has also claimed national status as one of the first places to introduce Americans to this authentic, upscale version of Thai cuisine, far from the Americanized pad thai and peanut-sauce-drenched dishes prevalent throughout the city and country.

Originally opening in a tiny six-table storefront, Sampanthavivat relocated down the street a couple years later to a larger but still relatively intimate space. He's also helped elevate the once barren Albany Park neighborhood, which has seen a burgeoning Thai population over the years. Sampanthavivat has teamed up with local aldermen, architects, city planners, and investors to help redevelop the area, including rehabbing the former district police station for the Thai Town Center, a community center that will house a spa and wellness center, educational and cultural space, and Sampanthavivat's second restaurant and retail outlet, plus a public-access rooftop garden.

An academic at heart who writes poetry and composes music on the side, Sampanthavivat hails from the southern Thai province of Trang, where he grew up on his

family's rubber plantation. His literature studies eventually took him to the University of Chicago and other renowned institutions around the world.

With no background in the restaurant field, but armed with a talent for cooking, a willingness to do all jobs, and a vision, Sampanthavivat has earned dozens of awards. The menu, which features a constantly changing five-course tasting menu as well as family-style, traditional "Thai banquet" dishes and a handful of his own creations thrown in, spans the regions of Sampanthavivat's native country, including urban Bangkok fare and country cooking in more sophisticated renditions.

The artistry in Sampanthavivat's plating—he's been called a master of vegetable carvery in the vein of classical French chefs—is echoed in the dining room, decorated with traditional Thai paintings by his younger brother, Anawat, including a rainbow-colored three-wall mural intricately depicting stories of the Buddha that took almost a year to finish.

Here Sampanthavivat shares his recipe for hung lay curry, one of northern Thailand's most important curry dishes, he says, which is eaten both as a daily meal and on all festive occasions. With plenty of ginger and turmeric, the dish represents a classic Burmese-style curry, yet brightened by fresh herbs and lemongrass. Choose a skinless pork belly—five-layer pork, the Chinese call it. Then, Sampanthavivat says, take your time. Slow-cooking this curry will result in a much richer flavor and tender pork that melts like butter.

HUNG LAY CURRY
(TURMERIC-MARINATED PORK CURRY)
(Serves 8–10)

For the pork, the marinade, and the chile paste:

3 pounds lean, skinless pork belly, cut into 3-inch squares
½ cup plus 2 tablespoons corn oil, divided
½ teaspoon sweet soy sauce
1½ teaspoons salt, divided
2 tablespoons chopped cilantro leaves, divided
2 tablespoons minced fresh ginger root, divided
¼ cup minced fresh turmeric root, divided
15 garlic cloves, minced, divided
3 shallots, minced, divided
10 dried guajillo chile peppers, soaked in warm water for 30 minutes, drained
10 dried chile de arbol peppers, stems removed

For the stir-fry:

1 teaspoon curry powder or hung lay spices
1 teaspoon fish paste
1–2 cups cold water or chicken stock, as needed
¾ cup palm sugar
3–4 teaspoons fish sauce
1 teaspoon paprika
1 cup tamarind juice
2 lemongrass stalks, white part only, crushed
6–7 kaffir lime leaves (bai makrude), torn into pieces

First, marinate the pork belly. In a resealable plastic bag or a bowl, combine pork with ½ cup oil, ½ teaspoon soy sauce, 1 teaspoon salt, 1 tablespoon cilantro, and half each of the ginger, turmeric, garlic, and shallots. Cover and refrigerate for at least 1 hour.

Meanwhile, prepare the chile paste. In a blender or food processor, add the guajillo and chile de arbol peppers, the remaining 1/2 teaspoon salt, and the remaining turmeric, garlic, shallot, and cilantro. Blend until smooth. Alternatively, pound ingredients to a paste in a mortar and pestle. Set aside.

Heat remaining 2 tablespoons oil in a large skillet over medium-high heat. Drain pork, discarding marinade. Toss pork with the chile paste, curry powder, and fish paste, tossing to combine. Partially cook the pork, tossing occasionally, about

5 minutes or until slightly firm to the touch. Add water or chicken stock, 1 tablespoon at a time, as necessary to prevent scorching.

Add palm sugar, fish sauce, paprika, tamarind juice, and lemongrass. Cover and simmer over medium-low heat until pork is fork tender, about 2–3 hours. Pour in enough stock or water to cover pork, if needed.

Divide curry into 8–10 bowls. Top with lime leaves and remaining freshly minced ginger. Serve with jasmine rice or sticky rice.

POULTRY

Serious, old-school restaurant critics and food connoisseurs would say never order chicken breast at a restaurant or face the dreaded dryness, one tough, bland bite at a time. Nowadays, with better access to smaller-production family farms and other sustainably raised protein sources, chefs have many more options when it comes not just to chicken but also eggs and other poultry.

At T.J.'S Free-Range Pastured Poultry, farmers Tim and Julie Ifft make sure their chickens have access to fresh, clean pasture and protection from harsh weather that includes strong sun and heat as well as snow and cold. They also protect their laying hens for fresh eggs and rotate the pastures to raise turkeys on natural grass for harvest in the fall. A handful of other farmers, such as John Caveny, specialize in hard-to-find heritage breed turkeys. Then there are the hunting birds of the Midwest, from duck to quail, squab, pheasant, even pigeon. The result of all this? More tender, better tasting, juicier meat, plus richer, more nutritious eggs, and plenty of environmental and social consciousness to go around.

As fried chicken and other comfort food staples have made a comeback, chefs are both keeping it class and putting on their own creative spins, from Ina's award-winning Southern-style chicken to Kobe-stuffed wings at one sixtyblue. And celebrity chef Rick Bayless, who more than a decade ago introduced the then-unusual combination of duck and tacos, has seen the dish, in all its various forms, become a staple on the menu at Frontera Grill. Next door, at Bayless's XOCO, wood-roasted chicken from Gunthorp Farms in Indiana forms the stuffing for one of the menu's most popular tortas.

ONE SIXTYBLUE

1400 West Randolph Street, West Loop
(312) 850-0303
www.onesixtyblue.com
Owner-Proprietor: Michael Jordan
Managing Company: Cornerstone Restaurant Group
Executive Chef: Michael McDonald

Michael Jordan was a legendary basketball star. But he is also a successful restaurateur. Since one sixtyblue opened at the edge of Randolph's Restaurant Row in the West Loop, the semi-fine-dining restaurant and lively bar space has changed dramatically, from its managing company to its chefs to the food and the feel. Martial Noguier, most recently the executive chef at Café des Architectes (page 185) first made a name for both himself and the restaurant, earning accolades from critics near and far during his eight-year reign. He handed over the keys to Midwestern-born Michael McDonald, who learned an appreciation of local foods as a young boy when he helped out on his grandfather's farm. McDonald has brought to one sixtyblue an approach that is markedly different from his predecessor's, reintroducing age-old comfort food classics that are more Midwestern and American-inspired than French, though he spent years training under fine-dining French master Jean Joho (Everest, page 166).

Still, since his takeover McDonald has maintained the same sophistication in the dining room that the restaurant's longtime regulars crave. That has translated into such dishes as a bright and clean soup of spring ramps enriched by a local farm egg and house-cured pork belly, alongside a rhubarb-glazed Slagel Farm chicken roasted with wheat berries, golden raisins, and baby bok choy also from the farmers' market.

Up front in the bar, McDonald has let loose a little more, introducing weekly special dinners like burgers and beer or bourbon and barbecue that have helped bring in a slightly younger crowd and breathe new life into the space. The Kobe beef stuffed wings have grown to be a favorite among this crowd, both for their uniqueness and for their deliciousness alongside a hoppy, bubbly brew. Unfortunately, one sixtyblue has closed, but that doesn't diminish this recipe. The space is being renovated for a new-concept restaurant.

KOBE CHICKEN WING SLIDERS
(Serves 12)

12 chicken wings
8 ounces ground Kobe beef
Pinch of freshly ground black pepper and kosher
　salt
1 egg
¼ cup milk
1 cup all-purpose flour
1 teaspoon cayenne pepper
2–3 cups vegetable oil
¼ cup barbecue sauce (preferably Michael
　Jordan's BBQ Sauce)
12 slices jalapeño-jack cheese
12 mini brioche buns, slit

Using a sharp knife, make a slit in along the chicken wing from top to bottom tip and remove the smaller bone, leaving the larger drumette bone.

Season the beef with salt and pepper and divide into 12 equal portions. Stuff each chicken wing with the meat. Secure by wrapping one side of the chicken skin over the other, stretching as much as possible.

To bread the wings, set out two shallow bowls. In one, whisk together the egg and milk. In the other, mix the flour and cayenne pepper. Dredge each chicken wing in the flour mixture, shaking off the excess. Dip in the egg mixture and then back in the flour. Set the breaded wings aside on a sheet tray.

Preheat oven to 400°F. Heat oil in a large skillet over medium-high heat. Add half of the chicken wings and fry until golden brown, about 3 minutes on each side. Repeat, adding more oil for the second batch if needed. As the wings are removed from the oil, transfer them to an oven-safe dish or pan and toss with barbecue sauce. Bake for 5–7 minutes or until crispy.

Remove wings from oven, top each with a cheese slice, and return to oven for an additional 1–2 minutes, or until cheese is melted and slightly bubbly. Slide one chicken wing into each bun. Serve immediately.

Ina's

1235 West Randolph Street, West Loop
(312) 226-8227
www.breakfastqueen.com
Chef-Owner: Ina Pinkney

A few things come to mind when thinking about Ina Pinkney: brunch, salt and pepper shakers, fried chicken, hotcakes, smiles and laughter. Known as the Breakfast Queen of Chicago, Pinkney became associated with salt and pepper shakers not long after she opened her first restaurant, Ina's Kitchen, in 1991 on Webster Avenue and bought a few funky pairs. Her customers saw a trend and began bringing fun new shakers, from chef characters to mermaids, cows and other animals, toaster ovens, fruits and vegetables.

Pinkney later closed that outpost, reopening in 2001 as simply Ina's at the edge of Restaurant Row in the West Loop. The salt and pepper shakers continued to flow in. And while they add to that charm that Ina's has always had, the shakers tend to go unused. It's not because the food is salty. It's because the food is consistently delicious, every time. Pinkney is one of those old-school restaurateurs with a cult following that spans decades.

When it comes to the smiles and laughter, Pinkney isn't stuck in the kitchen, she's out front in the dining room, making her rounds, giving hugs, refilling coffee mugs, and generally showing her spirit for the business and for everyone who's come to know and love her.

In her latest endeavors, Pinkney has become something of a community activist, to say the least. Frequently featured in the press and involved in speaking engagements,

conferences, television appearances, and other activities, she counts among her greatest accomplishments the cofounding of the Green Chicago Restaurant Co-op in 2007 with fellow restaurateur Dan Rosenthal. The nonprofit organization recognizes restaurants and other food businesses in the Chicago area that are doing their part to sustain the local economy, their own sector, and the environment, and that have third-party certifications to back up their claims. Some of those sustainable initiatives involve supporting local farmers and producers, something Pinkney has done for years.

Pinkney's hotcakes—"Heavenly Hots"—are as light and fluffy as clouds, flattened and rounded, then browned and slightly crisp around the edges. The fried chicken is also light, with a crisp, grease-free breading and served Southern style with crunchy, buttery waffles. Fried chicken is available in a gluten-free version using rice flours and tapioca starch. Oh, and the deep fryers are eco-friendly, energy-efficient, and filled with only trans-fat-free oil, of course. That's Ina, always looking out for her people and the environment. Here Pinkney has generously donated her chicken recipe, and one for her just-as-popular pasta frittata. Eat them separately or together, breakfast, lunch, or dinner.

INA'S AWARD-WINNING FRIED CHICKEN
(Serves 4)

For the chicken marinade:

1 3–3½-pound chicken, preferably natural or
   organic
1 quart buttermilk
1 teaspoon garlic powder
1 teaspoon kosher salt
1 teaspoon freshly ground black pepper
3 quarts trans-fat-free oil (Ina's uses canola)

For the coating:

2 cups all-purpose flour
2 teaspoons garlic powder
1 teaspoon kosher salt
1 teaspoon freshly ground black pepper

Cut the chicken into 8 serving pieces: 2 legs,
2 thighs, 2 wings, 2 breast halves. Reserve the
back for making soup or stock.Wash the chicken
and trim any visible fat. Combine buttermilk,
garlic powder, salt, and pepper. Place chicken
in a 1-gallon resealable plastic bag or large bowl
and pour in the seasoned buttermilk. Close the
bag or cover bowl. Refrigerate at least 2 hours or
overnight.

Heat oil in a heavy 6-quart pot over medium heat
to 250°F. While oil is heating, remove the chicken
from the bag and place on a rack to drain.

For coating, combine flour, garlic powder, salt, and
pepper in a pie tin or dish. Dredge chicken pieces
in flour mixture, turning and pressing to coat well.
Shake off any excess flour. Re-dredge if any part
is missing coverage.

Slowly and carefully lower the chicken into the hot
oil, skin side up, using tongs. Fry for 10 minutes
undisturbed, then turn the pieces gently to keep
them separated.

Cooking time for wings: 13–15 minutes; legs:
15–17 minutes; thighs: 18–20 minutes; breasts:
20–25 minutes. Chicken is done when internal
temperature reaches 160°F. If you're not sure
the chicken is done, use the tip of a sharp knife
and poke to see if the juices run clear. Serve with
waffles and pure maple syrup.

Ina's Pasta Frittata
(Serves 8–10)

2 tablespoons olive oil
¾ cup chopped onion
2 cloves garlic, minced
¾ cup thinly sliced red bell pepper
1½ cups sliced mushrooms
1½ cups thick-julienned zucchini
1 teaspoon dried oregano
Salt and freshly ground black pepper, to taste
10 extra-large eggs
¾ cup whole milk
1½ teaspoons salt
1 teaspoon freshly ground black pepper
1½ cups shredded sharp white cheddar cheese
½ cup grated Parmesan cheese
1 pound cream cheese
3 cups cooked spaghetti, drained and cooled

Heat oven to 350°F. Brush a 10-inch round cake pan or leakproof springform pan lightly with oil. Cut a piece of parchment paper to size and place in bottom of pan. Brush again with oil and set aside.

Sauté onion and garlic in olive oil until softened. Add red pepper, mushrooms, and zucchini. Continue to sauté until soft. Stir in oregano, salt, and pepper and set aside. (If the vegetables have given off a lot of liquid, drain before adding to the spaghetti.)

In large bowl of electric mixer, beat eggs, milk, salt, and pepper on low speed. Blend in cheddar and Parmesan cheeses. When combined and with machine running, add cream cheese, pulled by hand into bite-size bits.

Place cooked spaghetti into prepared pan. Spoon cooked vegetables over spaghetti. Pour in the egg mixture; mix with your hands so that all components are evenly distributed within the pan. Pat down so that solids are covered with liquid as much as possible.

Bake 30–40 minutes until firm to the touch and lightly brown. The frittata will puff up, then settle when cool. Remove from pan. Cut and serve immediately, or refrigerate and cut into portions the next day, reheating for 12–15 minutes at 400°F. Serve on a bed of lightly seasoned tomato sauce, and pass some grated Parmesan to sprinkle on top.

Frontera Grill / Topolobampo / XOCO

445 North Clark Street, River North
(312) 661-1434
www.fronterakitchens.com
Owner–Executive Chef: Rick Bayless

If Diana Kennedy is the abuela or grandmother of authentic Mexican cuisine in the United States, Rick Bayless is the abuelo of fine-dining Mexican. Now a household name, revered both domestically and abroad, Bayless first learned and loved authentic Mexican cuisine by studying Latin American culture at the University of Oklahoma, and later while working on a doctorate in anthropological linguistics at the University of Michigan.

But it wasn't until he traveled and lived in Mexico with his wife, business partner, and "rock" Deann that he truly understood and became passionate about its people and cuisine. During a recent trip to central Mexico, his zeal could be witnessed firsthand when Bayless lit up like a kid in a candy store at the small town's open-air market, enthusiastically explaining different ingredients and thinking up ways to use them for a cooking demonstration later that afternoon. Even in this rural Mexico town, many fans ran up to greet him.

Bayless grew up working in his parents' barbecue restaurant in Oklahoma City. So it wasn't a surprise that he turned to a life of cooking and restaurant ownership. But before that, he'd become an author, developing the masterpiece that is *Authentic Mexican: Regional Cooking from the Heart of Mexico* with Deann. Mexican cooking sealed the deal. Bayless ultimately moved to Chicago, where he opened Frontera Grill in 1987 and, two years later, the more fine-dining focused Topolobampo next door, becoming one of the most celebrated chefs in the nation.

At a time when fine dining in Chicago was predominantly French, Bayless asked, why not Mexican—the same techniques used in regional Mexican cooking, elevated by preciseness, creativity, and artfulness in plating and presentation. It was and is still a team effort in the kitchens at Topolobampo and Frontera Grill, which for eleven years included right-hand man and chef de cuisine Brian Enyart, who recently stepped down. Everything is talked about, ideas shared, tested, tweaked, and tested some more before ever hitting the menu, especially at fine-dining Topolobampo. Nothing is hurried, nothing is just OK or passable. At the same time, all the food is approachable and accessible to everyone. These are the first restaurants of their kind, not just for Chicago but for the country. It's no wonder lines form outside the restaurants well before the doors open and prime-time reservations can take months to get.

But Bayless isn't just a chef, he's an educator at heart. While researching for his book, he hosted a television series on regional Mexican cooking. Now he continues his television work, producing and hosting the PBS series *Mexico: One Plate at a Time,* often cooking, traveling, and teaching alongside daughter Lanie, with whom he's also coauthored a book. Outside of that, Bayless continues to host demonstrations, lectures, and other events geared toward teaching the everyday American consumer about Mexican culture and cuisine. There was once a time when average home cooks couldn't buy a jalapeño in Chicago, and even if they could, they wouldn't know what to do with one. Now that seems impossible to imagine, and it's fair to say that Bayless had something to do with it.

One of the endeavors Bayless has said he's most proud of is his establishment of the Frontera Farmer Foundation, a charitable organization dedicated to supporting Chicago-area family farms. Bayless has been a longtime supporter of "the little guy" when it comes to ingredient sourcing and supplying, and this extends back to the late eighties and early nineties. "I was fortunate to have someone like Rick be so encouraging and supportive," says Tracey Vowell of Three Sisters Garden in Kankakee, Illinois, who managed both restaurant kitchens for six years and slowly made the transition to farming. "I had to make sure I had a stable income throughout the change, and Rick was interested in keeping me around and using products from the farm. Rick was very kind the way he let me sort of wander off—it was a good relationship."

Bayless is a grower too, planting his own herbs, vegetables, and fruits in his home's expansive garden for his personal use as well as for the restaurant. Then there are the

charitable activities, the endless cookbooks, and the line of jarred salsas, seasonings, and more under the Frontera Foods label, a business venture Deann Bayless started and continues to run. It's a restaurant enterprise that shows no signs of slowing down anytime soon.

That includes Bayless's latest concept, XOCO, a street-food-focused carryout and casual dine-in eatery next to Topolobampo that was an instant success when it opened in 2009 with a menu heavy on breakfast and lunch tortas and soups, all made with locally sourced foods, of course. On top of that, Bayless still found time to participate on Bravo! TV's *Top Chef Masters* show and win. The Top Chef Master title really does say it all.

CARNITAS DE PATO (CHUNKS OF DUCK MEAT) WITH CRUNCHY TOMATILLO-AVOCADO SALSA

(Makes 3 generous cups of carnitas and 2½ cups of salsa)

For the duck carnitas:

6 large duck legs (about 2½–3 pounds total)
4 teaspoons salt
2 teaspoons dried oregano, preferably Mexican
2 tablespoons freshly squeezed lime juice
6 cups fresh lard
8 garlic cloves, peeled and halved

For the tomatillo-avocado salsa:

4 medium tomatillos, husks removed and rinsed
½ cup loosely packed, coarsely chopped cilantro
2 small serrano chiles, stemmed and roughly
    chopped
¼ cup water
1 ripe avocado, peeled and pitted
1 small white onion, cut into ¼-inch dice
¾ teaspoon salt, or to taste

For serving:

Fresh tortillas*

First, marinate the duck. Lay the legs in a 13 x 9-inch nonaluminum baking dish. Season on both sides with the salt, oregano, and lime juice. Cover and refrigerate for at least an hour, up to overnight.

Preheat the oven to 300°F. In a large (4-quart) saucepan, melt the lard. Remove the duck from the baking dish and pat dry with paper towels. Rinse and dry the baking dish. Replace the legs in the dish and cover with melted lard, submerging completely. Scatter the garlic cloves over the duck, nestling them into the lard. Slide into the oven (on a rimmed baking sheet to avoid spills), and bake for about 2 hours, or until duck is very tender. Cool to lukewarm.

Meanwhile, make the salsa. Roughly chop 2 of the tomatillos and scoop them into a food processor with the cilantro and chiles. Pour in ¼ cup water and process to a slushy, coarse puree. Roughly chop half the avocado, add it to the processor, and pulse until it is incorporated into the salsa. Scrape into a serving dish. Rinse diced onion in cold water, drain, and add to the salsa. Finely chop the remaining tomatillos and add to salsa. Finally, chop the remaining avocado into ¼-inch pieces and stir them into the salsa, along with the salt.

Once duck is cool anough, remove from the lard. Pull off the skin and set aside. Pull off the meat in large pieces, discarding the bones. In a very large (12-inch) skillet, heat 2 tablespoons of the lard over medium-high heat. When lard is hot but not smoking, add the duck skin and cook, turning frequently, until very crisp, about 5 minutes. Remove and drain on paper towels. Next, add the meat and cook, turning regularly, until browned and crisping in spots, about 7 or 8 minutes. Drain on paper towels. Scoop onto a serving platter, coarsely crumbling the duck skin over the top. Serve with the tomatillo-avocado salsa and warm tortillas.

***Note:** While homemade tortillas are ideal, to quickly warm store-bought tortillas without drying them out, Bayless recommends wrapping a small stack in a damp towel or damp paper towel and microwaving for 30 seconds on full power. Transfer tortillas to a tortilla warmer. These warmers can be made out of ceramic, stone, plastic, or hand-woven straw and/or cloth, some versions of which are also microwave friendly.

MEXICANS IN CHICAGO

Chicago has the second-largest population of Mexicans outside Mexico, behind only Los Angeles. You wouldn't think so, given the city's distance from the border, but a large majority of Mexicans living and working in Chicago come from the state of Michoacán, according to the Mexico Tourism Board. Rolling, grassy hills, temperate climate, and vast avocado orchards characterize Michoacán, meaning "many lakes," which is also the translation of the Native American word "Michigan." This and its location in the "heartland" of the country have led Michoacán to be compared to the U.S. Midwest.

Surprisingly, the Mexican Tourism Board says American employment ranks above avocados as the highest grossing source of revenue for Michoacán, even though the region is the largest producer of Haas avocados in the world. By "American employment" the board means men traveling to the States to work and send money back to their families.

Chicago's Mexican workforce is due mainly to one thing: the city's bounty of restaurants. Michoacán natives are food-focused, cooking often and cooking well. So it's no wonder that many travel to Chicago to work the hot lines in the thousands of kitchens here. Indeed, many Mexican immigrants have worked their way up to top posts in the kitchen, such as Noe Sanchez of Convito Café (page 41), who started in the dish room and ultimately became executive chef. Maria Concannon of Don Juan (page 128) came to the States from Mexico City and has established a legacy of authentic Mexican cooking in Chicago.

While not an immigrant himself, Iron Chef America and Chicago native Jose Garces of Mercat a la Planxa (page 106) provides full health-care benefits and a retirement plan for his workers, many of whom he says are from Mexico and have remained loyal to him for almost a decade.

Without this hard-working, skilled, and reliable group of Mexican immigrants, many Chicago restaurants wouldn't survive. And without this food-loving, family-focused group, Chicago wouldn't be the rich, culturally diverse, warm and exciting place it is. Chicago, frankly, just wouldn't be Chicago.

THE SIGNATURE ROOM AT THE 95TH

JOHN HANCOCK CENTER
875 NORTH MICHIGAN AVENUE, MAG MILE
(312) 787-9596
WWW.SIGNATUREROOM.COM
OWNERS: RICK ROMAN AND NICK PYKNIS
FORMER EXECUTIVE CHEF: PATRICK SHEERIN

Amazing views, top-rated service, and plenty of birthdays, engagements, anniversaries, first dates, and fiftieth dates. The Signature Room at the 95th floor of the Chicago skyline icon John Hancock Center has a reputation for being a special place. But the food has become more special every year, as longtime chef Patrick Sheerin has moved from banquets to running the kitchen over the last eight and a half years, and lately has expanded his relationships with Midwestern farmers and producers.

"We're not just seasonal, we've become really market driven," he says, noting the frequently changing menu and monthly special dinners. The restaurant also donates proceeds to a charity of the month, including many farm-focused organizations such as the Land Connection and children-focused groups geared toward autism and cancer research.

"Going forward, we're trying for more refinement and professionalism both in cooking and in service, and looking to bring fine dining back a bit—we got away from it a little during the recession," says Sheerin.

Sourcing humanely raised, sustainably produced meat is another focus of Sheerin's.

"We feel it's better for the flavor. The muscles aren't stressed, and the animals develop better by being on pasture and eating different types of grains and grasses that are a natural part of their environment," he says. "We're trying to change the bar here with this issue. There are a lot of chefs in this city, especially, who definitely have elevated the expectations and demand for more humanely, sustainably raised protein."

For his roast chicken at the restaurant, Sheerin uses chicken from Gunthorp Farms in Indiana and other Midwestern sustainable farms where possible, but if local farm chicken isn't available, look for meat stamped with humanely raised certification for the most tender, juicy, and socially conscious option.

CRISPY-ROASTED CHICKEN WITH CREAMY GRITS AND KING MUSHROOMS
(Serves 2)

For the chicken:

1 whole chicken, 3–4 pounds
3 tablespoons unsalted butter

For the grits:

2 cups water
2 cups whole milk
1 cup uncooked grits
2 tablespoons unsalted butter
Dash of Tabasco or other hot sauce
Salt and freshly ground black pepper, to taste
¼ cup finely grated Parmesan cheese

For the brown butter roasting jus:

2 sticks (8 ounces) unsalted butter
3 tablespoons powdered milk
1 medium carrot, peeled and diced
1 celery rib, sliced into ½-inch pieces
1 small onion, diced
3 sprigs fresh thyme
½ cup dry sherry
¼ cup mirin
¼ cup sherry vinegar
4 cups chicken stock or low-sodium chicken broth

For the mushrooms and garnish:

2 large king oyster mushrooms, cleaned
3 tablespoons unsalted butter
1 shallot, thinly sliced
3 cloves garlic, thinly sliced
2 sprigs fresh thyme, roughly chopped
2 tablespoons thinly sliced parsley

Preheat the oven to 300°F. Cut up the chicken. Split the breast into two halves, and bone the thighs, leaving the skin on. Reserve the rest of the chicken parts and carcass to make the brown butter roasting jus.

Melt 3 tablespoons butter in a large skillet. Cook over medium-low heat until slightly browned and nutty, about 5 minutes. Add breast halves and thighs, skin side down. Place skillet in oven to bake for 45 minutes. Remove chicken from pan; set aside on stovetop. Cover to keep warm.

For the grits, in a medium-size sauté pan, bring the water and milk to a boil. Whisk in the grits. Continue to whisk until the grits come to a boil. Cover the pot with a lid and place in the 300°F oven. Cook the grits for approximately 1 hour, checking the consistency every 15 minutes. Whisk smooth if needed. Stir in butter and hot sauce. Season to taste with salt and pepper; set aside.

For the brown butter roasting jus, heat 2 tablespoons butter in the same skillet used for the chicken breast and thighs over medium heat. Chop the chicken parts and carcass and cook until caramelized, about 10 minutes. Pour about ¼ cup of the juices into a separate saucepan, add the powdered milk, and bring to a simmer over medium-high heat. Cook until well incorporated, about 3 minutes. Set aside. Add the carrot, celery, onion, and thyme to the first pan with the chicken carcass, continuing to caramelize. Deglaze the pan with sherry, mirin, and sherry vinegar. Reduce to almost a thick glaze, then add the chicken stock. Simmer until the liquid is reduced by half. Strain liquid from the pan into a blender, discarding the chicken and vegetables (can be saved for later soup making). Add the cooked powdered milk mixture to the blender and process until smooth.

For the king oyster mushrooms, score stems about ⅛-inch deep to flatten. Heat 3 tablespoons butter over medium heat. Add shallot and garlic and cook until shallot is translucent and garlic is fragrant and lightly browned, about 2–3 minutes. Add mushrooms; cook until mushrooms have released their juices and are tender and slightly browned, about 5 minutes. Glaze mushroom mixture lightly with about a tablespoon of the brown butter chicken jus. Remove from heat; stir in thyme. Set aside.

To serve, warm the grits over the stovetop, adding a little bit of milk if necessary. The grits should be fairly firm, not runny. Fold in Parmesan cheese. To crisp the chicken, heat a cast-iron skillet over medium-high heat. When hot, add the chicken pieces and cook until skin is crisp, turning occasionally, about 2–3 minutes. Spoon grits in a dollop in the center of each plate. Place chicken thigh and chicken breast around the grits; top with half of the mushrooms. Repeat with remaining chicken and mushrooms for the second plate. Spoon the brown butter jus over the chicken on both plates, taking care not to pour on the grits. Garnish with parsley.

Le Colonial

937 North Rush Street, Gold Coast
(312) 255-0088
www.lecolonialchicago.com
Executive Chef: Chan Le

This French-Vietnamese institution in Chicago's Gold Coast neighborhood is a celebrity-sighting jackpot. Countless stars, from actors and musicians to politicians and other movers and shakers, have taken seats here, both inside and out on the charming sidewalk patio during fairer weather months. Le Colonial's winning combination of good food and literally dramatic ambience in a prime location has kept it alive through growing competition, recessions, and other typical restaurant challenges.

Tucked in between nightclubs, big scenester restaurants, and trendy boutiques on this busy stretch of Rush Street, Le Colonial sits just south of the Rush and State Street intersection, infamously known as the "Viagra Triangle," which earned its nickname from the many affluent, luxury-car-driving men seeking women in the area.

Le Colonial stands apart from the rest of this street as a quiet, serene oasis, thanks to a bright and breezy dining room with tall green ferns, light ivory walls covered in mirrors, and French doors that open on warm days. When it comes to the menu, many say Le Colonial was the first of its kind in the city, serving a fine-dining version of the Vietnamese classics typically found farther north in Little Vietnam (See Asians in Chicago, page 130), elevated by high-quality ingredients and gorgeous, almost sultry plating. The Ca Chien Saigon, crispy seared whole red snapper, and Sup Do Bien, a Vietnamese fish stew in a lemongrass saffron broth, rank as the most popular dishes. Here chef Chan Le offers a recipe for another lemongrass-broth–based dish typically found in Vietnamese cuisine.

Ga Xao Xa Ot
(Spicy Lemongrass Chicken)
(Serves 3)

10 ounces sliced chicken breast
2 tablespoons cornstarch
¼ cup canola oil, divided
2 portobello caps, cleaned
3 tablespoons fish sauce
4½ teaspoons oyster sauce
2 tablespoons sugar
1 stalk lemongrass, bottom only, sliced*
2 cloves garlic, chopped
¾ teaspoon red chile pepper flakes
6 Asian basil leaves, stacked, rolled into
    a cigar shape, and thinly sliced

Preheat the oven to 350°F.

Combine the chicken, cornstarch, and 2 tablespoons of the oil in a resealable plastic bag or bowl to marinate. Refrigerate.

Brush portobello caps lightly with 1 tablespoon oil and roast in the oven for 15 minutes. When cool enough to handle, slice caps into 1½-inch pieces and set aside.

Next, prepare the sauce. Combine the fish and oyster sauces and sugar in a small bowl; set aside.

Heat 1 tablespoon oil in a wok or deep sauté pan over medium-high heat. When oil begins to shimmer, add the chicken and cook, tossing frequently, until browned and almost cooked through, about 4–5 minutes. Add the lemongrass, garlic, and red pepper flakes and cook until fragrant, tossing frequently, about 1 minute. Add the portobello caps and the sauce. Continue to cook, tossing frequently until liquid has reduced

slightly, about another 1–2 minutes. Garnish with basil and serve.

Note: To prepare the lemongrass, first cut off the top two-thirds, the green part, leaving about a 4-inch white-only stalk. Next, make a thin slit down the stalk and peel away the tough outer layers. Slice the remaining stalk into 1/4-inch pieces.

Cyrano's Bistrot/Cyrano's Cafe and

Cyrano's Bistrot
546 North Wells Street, River North
(312) 467-0546
www.cyranosbistrot.com

Cyrano's Cafe and Wine Bar on the Riverwalk
233 East Lower Wacker Drive, Loop
(312) 616-1400
www.cyranosbistrot.com
Chef-Owner: Didier Durand

Didier Durand opened Cyrano's Bistrot, his first restaurant since leaving the multi-starred Carlos in Highland Park in 1996, naming it after the fictional, troubled romancer Cyrano de Bergerac, who was from the same hometown as Durand. Located in the southwest region of France, Bergerac is known for rich wines, earthy truffles, trout, escargots, and fois gras.

Ah, fois gras, a buttery lobe of serenity and pleasure in the eyes of so many food lovers, including Durand. But the spreadable duck liver was also the source of a hotly contested political battle in Chicago. In 2006 fiery PETA activists began to challenge the force-feeding operations that often go into raising duck for liver fattening, and some city aldermen took notice. In a shocking occurrence, the city council voted to ban the sale of fois gras within city limits. Many chefs, including Durand, rebelled.

Some continued to serve mini fois gras pieces legally, for free, as amuse-bouches and other complimentary starter courses. Doug Sohn of Hot Doug's, known famously for a fois-gras-topped dog, willingly accepted fines in sacrifice for the sacred delicacy. Durand spoke out in city council meetings and other venues, held fundraisers, and worked to bring chefs together in a fight back. Former mayor Richard M. Daley also criticized the brouhaha, urging aldermen to focus on more pressing matters of government, such as improving the city's schools and fighting crime. Point taken.

After two years, plenty of backlash, and a sense that Illinois government was becoming a laughingstock (an ousted governor didn't help), the city council reversed the ban. Foodies and chefs rejoiced. Still, the ban and all its surrounding activities did spark a new debate—we should better understand our food and demand that the animals we eat be treated better.

Now fois gras is back on the menu, and Durand even erected a "fois gras museum" in the restaurant, complete with photos and historic documents. Also on the menu is an eclectic mix of classic French bistro dishes and more contemporary creations, paired with a slew of hard-to-find wines from Bergerac.

In summer Durand's second outpost, Cyrano's Cafe on the Riverwalk, opens up. Set along the Chicago River underneath busy Wacker Drive and surrounded by trees and a new garden Durand put in, the experience is like a

Monet garden painting, with the addition of diners eating and drinking at bistro tables. Though the walk-up service "bar" is more like a little shack, a focal point is the outdoor smoker, where Durand has spit-roasted whole suckling pigs for special dinners and events.

Here Durand offers a new take on a classic French bistro dish, personalized by his use of duck confit and lamb. The trick with cassoulet, he says, is to be patient—partially cook the ingredients separately to bring out their natural flavors, and then let them caramelize and meld in a leisurely braise. Next, take a spoon and a big bowl, and enjoy.

Cassoulet of Duck, Lamb, and Sausage

(Serves 8)

1 pound dried navy beans, soaked overnight
    in cold water
8 cups chicken stock or broth, divided
1 bay leaf
1 teaspoon salt
1 teaspoon freshly ground black pepper
3 tablespoons olive oil or duck fat*, divided
4 duck legs
1 pound boneless leg of lamb, cut into 1-inch
    chunks
4 links pork sausage (about 1 pound)
    (can also use merguez, blood sausage,
    and/or venison sausage)
8 strips bacon, chopped
1 small carrot, peeled and diced
1 small leek, white parts only, sliced
4 cloves garlic, minced
2 shallots, minced
¼ cup tomato paste
2 ripe tomatoes, peeled, seeded, and quartered
2 cups dried bread crumbs

In a large pot, bring the navy beans, 6 cups chicken stock, and bay leaf to a boil. Reduce heat to medium, cover and simmer 45 minutes, or until beans are almost tender but still firm to the bite. Season with salt and pepper during the last 5 minutes of cooking. Turn off heat and set aside.

Preheat oven to 400°F.

Heat 1 tablespoon of the oil or duck fat in a large oven-safe pot over medium-high heat. Add duck legs and cook until crispy, about 5 minutes a side. Remove from pot and set aside.

Add 1 more tablespoon oil or duck fat and cook lamb pieces until browned on all sides, about 7–10 minutes total. Remove and set aside.

Add remaining tablespoon of olive oil or duck fat and cook sausages until browned on all sides, about 7–10 minutes total. Remove and set aside.

Reduce heat to medium and add bacon pieces, carrot, leek, garlic, and shallots, cooking until soft, about 4 minutes. Add tomato paste and tomatoes. Continue to cook 1–2 more minutes, scraping up browned bits, until tomato liquid has evaporated slightly. Set mixture aside and allow to cool slightly.

In the same pot, using a slotted spoon, spread beans in an even layer along the bottom. Pour in remaining 2 cups stock or broth. Nestle in the duck legs, lamb pieces, and sausages. Cover and bake for 1 hour, or until sausages are cooked through.

Sprinkle bread crumbs on top and bake, uncovered, for an additional 10–15 minutes, or until crust is golden and the juices and fat are absorbed.

Serve cassoulet family-style, or divide equally among 8 deep bowls.

*Note: Duck fat can be purchased in many specialty grocery or butcher stores. Or make your own by sautéing duck breasts for another meal and saving the fat from the pan.

THE GAGE / HENRI

THE GAGE
24 SOUTH MICHIGAN AVENUE, THE LOOP
(312) 372-4243
WWW.THEGAGECHICAGO.COM

HENRI
18 SOUTH MICHIGAN AVENUE, THE LOOP
(312) 578-0763
WWW.HENRICHICAGO.COM
OWNER: BILLY LAWLESS
EXECUTIVE CHEF: DIRK FLANIGAN

At first glance, The Gage would seem like a modern-day Irish or English pub, and in some regards it is, with its loud, boisterous atmosphere, expansive mahogany bar, strong lineup of specialty beers, and after-work happy-hour crowd that puts other city bars to shame. But delve a bit further, into the kitchen specifically, and you'll find Dirk Flanigan at the helm, carefully plating dishes meant for real culinary enthusiasts, not just for beer-hungry patrons who may have had a little too much to drink.

Though The Gage has been called a gastropub of sorts (see Modern Gastropub, page 68), the title is only somewhat fair—Flanigan's creations far surpass that level of comfort food cooking. His style touches on the comfort, to be sure, with hearty game dishes, rich starters, and decadent desserts. But in a more refined approach, he elevates the classic Canadian poutine using elk meat and homemade curd cheese, and steak tartare becomes bison tartare with grainy mustard and cornichons. Further down the menu, seared scallops pair with cocoa nibs, cocoa butter, cinnamon-jalapeño relish, and orange browned butter for a sweet and savory dish. A wagyu sirloin steak joins with tart apple, aged cheddar, and smoked shallot vinaigrette.

Next door, at owner Billy Lawless's second outpost Henri, Flanigan spreads his artistic wings and gets into some really sophisticated cooking and plating, much more in line with his fine-dining background. In this much quieter, intimate, food-focused setting, which seems the antithesis of its big brother, Flanigan works his magic. The game hen recipe offered here, a twist on a classic French dish, draws on both restaurant styles—hearty game meat and Midwestern brussels sprouts from The Gage, with a delicate huckleberry gastrique and rich croquettes reminiscent of French-inspired Henri.

FRENCH GAME HEN WITH CROQUETTES, PUREE OF BRUSSELS SPROUTS, AND MUSHROOM-HUCKLEBERRY SAUCE

(Serves 2)

For the game hen and brine:

1 quart cold water
4 ounces chardonnay vinegar or
    white wine vinegar
6 whole juniper berries, crushed
1 shallot, minced
10 whole black peppercorns
1 garlic clove, minced
3 sprigs fresh marjoram, stemmed and chopped
1 whole game hen, cut into 2 bone-in breasts,
    2 legs, 2 wings, and 2 thighs
Olive oil

For the puree:

8 ounces fresh brussels sprouts, trimmed
¼ cup heavy cream

For the croquettes:

1 egg yolk
¼ cup heavy cream
1 small shallot, peeled
2 chives, sliced fine
Salt and freshly ground black pepper, to taste
½ cup fresh bread crumbs

For the mushroom-huckleberry sauce:

2 cups sliced crimini mushrooms
2 tablespoons white wine vinegar
½ cup turkey or chicken broth or stock
1½ cup huckleberries*
½ stick cold butter, cut into ½-inch cubes

For the brine, combine water, vinegar, juniper berries, shallot, peppercorns, garlic, marjoram, and hen breasts and thighs in a large bowl. Cover and refrigerate at least 2 hours or up to overnight.

For the puree, heat oven to 400°F. Blanch brussels sprouts in salted water for 30 seconds, drain, shock in an ice bath, and drain again. Roast brussels sprouts for 10 minutes. Place in a blender with cream and blend until pureed, 2–3 minutes, adding additional cream if necessary. Season with salt and set aside.

To prepare the croquettes, poach the hen legs and wings in simmering broth or water until meat is cooked through, about 15 minutes. Drain and cool. Remove meat from legs and wings, discarding the skin and bones. Place meat in a blender or food processor along with the yolk, cream, shallot, and chives. Process until well mixed. Season with salt and pepper. Chill mixture until cold.

Preheat oven to 375°F. Remove game hen breasts and thighs from the brine and dry with paper towel. Coat lightly with olive oil. Cook in an ovenproof skillet, skin side down, until well browned. Turn hen pieces skin side up and roast in oven for 12–14 minutes, or until meat is no longer pink.

Meanwhile, roll chilled croquette mixture into 1-inch balls, adding bread crumbs if mixture is too soft to hold together. Roll balls on a flat surface into 1½-inch-long cylinders. Coat thoroughly with bread crumbs. Pour oil into a skillet to a depth of 1 inch. Heat the oil over medium-high heat to 350°F. Fry croquettes, turning frequently, until browned and cooked through. Drain on paper towels.

To prepare the sauce, pour off all the oil from the skillet except for 1 tablespoon. Over medium-high heat, cook the mushrooms until they are lightly browned and juices are evaporated. Remove the mushrooms and set aside. Add the vinegar, scraping up any browned bits, then add the stock. Add the huckleberries and turn up heat, continuing to cook until stock reduces by half. Turn off heat and allow to cool slightly. Add the

butter, one piece at a time, until sauce is thick enough to coat the back of a spoon. Not all the butter may be needed. Once the sauce has thickened, stir the cooked mushrooms back in.

To serve, spoon brussels sprouts puree evenly onto two plates. Place the hen breast halves and thighs with the croquettes over the puree and spoon sauce around the plate.

Note: If huckleberries aren't available, use blackberries or tart blueberries.

Old Town Social

455 West North Avenue, Old Town
(312) 266-2277
www.oldtownsocial.com
Executive Chef: Jared Van Camp
Owners: Chris Dexter and Chris Freeman
Chef de Cuisine: Sam Burman

Old Town Social is first and foremost a bar. But it's a bar that happens to serve a rich and decadent pork belly Reuben sandwich, with meat that's been brined and smoked for twelve hours, alongside homemade sauerkraut.

Piggybacking on the "gastropub" theme, Jared Van Camp was recruited by nightlife veterans Chris Dexter and Chris Freeman to head up the kitchen at this vintage-style bar and lounge at the northernmost edge of the Old Town neighborhood. He quickly outshined any initially basic expectations he may have had. Going on to put this lounge on the map of serious culinary destinations in the city, he also helped lead the "house-made everything" trend that continues today, namely house-made salumi, sausages, and other charcuterie. Declared a rising star by various media outlets, Van Camp has also joined the small group of chefs including Rob Levitt (Movers and Shakers, page 183) and Chris Pandel of The Bristol (page 124) geared toward using the whole animal, which entails bringing in whole pigs or sides of beef for in-house butchering and a no-fear approach to using offal.

In 2009 Van Camp left his post for San Diego, where he helped Dexter and Freeman open their second outpost, Quality Social. But he's back in Chicago now, and better than ever. A Paul Kahan and Rick Tramonto–trained chef, Van Camp brings his mastery of protein and his penchant for interesting flavor combinations to the table. Here Van Camp offers his secret harissa-spiced wings recipe, a clear favorite at Old Town Social, with a dipping sauce of cucumber-mint raita to cool each bite.

Harissa Duck Wings with Cucumber-Mint Raita

(Serves 6–8, with extra harissa)

For the duck wings:

5 pounds duck wing drumettes
2 tablespoons kosher salt
1 tablespoon sugar
5 cloves garlic, thinly sliced
10 sprigs fresh thyme
6 cups duck fat
Canola oil
2 cups all-purpose flour

For the harissa:

2 ounces dried chile de arbol peppers
2 ounces dried ancho peppers
4 ounces dried chipotle peppers
1 teaspoon caraway seeds, toasted
1 teaspoon coriander seeds, toasted
½ teaspoon cumin seeds, toasted
½ cup extra-virgin olive oil
5 garlic cloves, peeled
½ teaspoon salt, or to taste
¼ teaspoon sugar, or to taste
Dash freshly squeezed lemon juice
1 stick cold butter, cut into ½-inch cubes

For the cucumber-mint raita:

½ cucumber, peeled, seeded, and diced
1 shallot, minced
¼ cup chopped fresh cilantro
1 tablespoon chopped fresh mint
1 cup Greek-style yogurt
1 tablespoon freshly squeezed lime juice

First, cure the wings. Using a sharp knife or cleaver, chop about ½ inch off the narrow end of the drumettes. Mix together the drumettes with the salt, sugar, garlic, and thyme. Cover tightly with plastic wrap and refrigerate, at least 4–6 hours, up to overnight.

Preheat the oven to 275°F. In a large, heavy-bottomed pot, heat the duck fat over medium heat to 250°F. Carefully add the wings, cover, and transfer to the oven. Bake until wings are tender, about 4 hours.

Meanwhile, prepare the harissa. Fill a medium saucepan with water and bring to a boil. Remove from heat. In a dry skillet over medium-high heat, toast the chile de arbol, ancho, and chipotle chiles until softened and fragrant but not blackened. Discard stems and seeds. Add to the warm water. Cover and let sit for 20 minutes.

Finely grind the caraway, coriander, and cumin seeds in a blender or spice grinder. Set aside. Drain the chiles and place in a blender along with the spices, olive oil, garlic cloves, and a splash of water. Puree to a smooth paste. Season with salt, sugar, and lemon juice. Measure out ½ cup of the harissa paste and set aside. Cover and refrigerate remaining harissa for later use, up to two months.

Next, make the cucumber raita. In a medium bowl, mix the cucumber, shallot, cilantro, mint, yogurt, and lime juice. Cover and refrigerate.

Remove wings from the oven, allowing to cool slightly, uncovered. Drain the wings and transfer to a sheet tray until cool enough to handle. Reserve the fat, refrigerating or freezing for another use.

In the same pot used to bake the wings, add oil to a depth of 2 inches and heat to 350°F. Meanwhile, in a small saucepan over medium heat, warm the ½ cup harissa paste. Remove from heat, allowing to cool slightly. Stir in cold butter, a cube at a time, until smooth and velvety. Set aside.

To finish the wings, place flour in a large, shallow bowl. Working in batches, dredge wings in flour, shaking to remove exess, then lower carefully into the hot oil. Fry wings until golden and crispy, about 4–5 minutes. Drain on paper towels. In a large bowl, mix the wings with the warm harissa-butter mixture. Serve wings with cucumber-mint raita for dipping.

DESSERTS

The words "dessert" and "Chicago" when used together conjure up two names: Gale Gand and Mindy Segal. Both are considered pastry queens here and across the nation.

Gand started by laying the foundation for fine-dining desserts in Chicago, first as pastry chef at Trio and then as executive pastry chef of Tru, which she co-owns along with a handful of other concepts and creations in the area.

Segal followed close in those footsteps years later with Hot Chocolate, now Mindy's Hot Chocolate—a casual eatery devoted to both the sweet and the savory that has racked up numerous nominations and awards and showcased Segal's delicate and sophisticated, but also approachable and playful, touch.

Pastry chefs have an interesting post in the kitchen, often working in the quiet shadows of the executive chef, though they have a much greater stamp on the entire menu and kitchen than one would expect. More often than not, they'll work hand in hand with their savory cohorts, creating little masterpieces that pop up everywhere in addition to just the dessert menu. That could mean a crispy shortbread cookie underneath an oyster for an amuse-bouche, a fruited gastrique for rich fois gras, or soft pillows of meringue for a heavy meat dish.

And then, at meal's end, it becomes their turn to step out from behind the curtains and shine. Just as simple bread and butter can make or break a diner's first impression, it's the final bite that really seals the deal. First impressions entice. Last impressions determine whether one comes back for more.

TRU

686 NORTH SAINT CLAIR STREET, STREETERVILLE
(312) 202-0001
WWW.TRURESTAURANT.COM
OWNER: LETTUCE ENTERTAIN YOU
PARTNER-EXECUTIVE PASTRY CHEF: GALE GAND
EXECUTIVE CHEF: ANTHONY MARTIN

It's been argued that no other pastry chef in the country has earned such national and international stardom as Gale Gand—chef and pastry chef, restaurateur, cookbook author, TV personality, root beer brewer, cupcake dreamer, degreed artist, and devoted mom.

Gand is as multitalented as her resume shows, from creating imaginative, perfectly executed pastry creations at fine-dining institution Tru, to inspiring home bakers through her multiple cookbooks and as host of the former Food Network TV show Sweet Dreams, to bringing smiles to both kid and adult faces with her self-developed root beer and decadent creations at Patty Rothman's MORE Cupcakes, where she served as consulting chef.

"I didn't choose the pastry world, it sort of chose me," she says. "I was waitressing at a vegetarian restaurant while studying art in college, and one of the line cooks didn't show up one day. The owner said, 'Gale, can you cook?' I told him no, but he threw me in there anyway and said, 'You can now.'"

The rest was history. "I had this funny feeling, like a calm had come over me and I found this home," she says. In a natural progression from art on paper to art in the kitchen, Gand

quickly took an interest in cooking, striving first to be not a sweets but a savory chef. But when faced with a similar situation—an opening in pastry came up while she was working the garde manger station—Gand found herself in that role even though she viewed pastry as a "place where they stick women" and had wanted all along to stay with the guys on the hot line.

Pastry found its way to her heart as art once did. "It just fit me," Gand says. "I loved the chemistry and the physics of it all, but also the creativity that goes along with it. There is a lot of freedom and aesthetics and yet there are rules, like learning how to be an improvisational musician."

With the births of her son and twin daughters, Gand paid closer attention to the quality of foods she fed herself and her children—working with local farmers and producers to secure the best ingredients she could find before it was the cool thing to do. She also focused on creating both sweet and savory dishes that fell in line with the seasons, not only for better taste but to help preserve the earth.

Having children has also shaped Gand's latest endeavors teaching baking and classes at grammar schools and high schools as well as engaging in other educational outreach. On top of that, she continues to run Tru and M Burger, the quick-serve burger restaurant operating out of the restaurant's kitchen, as well as Tramonto Steak and Seafood in Wheeling. And she continues to write cookbooks, travel the nation and the world, and work on selling more of the Gale's Root Beer she started producing in small batches in 1993.

"The chef in me thinks, I'll sleep later, when I retire," Gand says. And that could be a while, she adds. For now, Gand offers a simple chocolate mousse recipe—easy to make, classic, and a winner every time. Her only advice: Use the best ingredients possible.

MOUSSE AU CHOCOLAT
(Serves 12)

8 ounces bittersweet chocolate,
   broken into small pieces
2 cups heavy cream
1 cup egg whites
1 cup sugar

Place the chocolate pieces in a bowl and set over simmering water or in the microwave for 1 minute. If microwaving, cook an additional 30 seconds if not melted.

In a stand mixer fitted with a whisk attachment, or using a handheld mixer, whip the cream until it forms stiff peaks. Scrape whipped cream into a separate bowl, cover, and refrigerate.

Add the whites to the mixer or bowl and whip until they form soft peaks. Drizzle in the sugar and continue whipping till glossy and the sugar has dissolved. Taste the mixture to make sure there is still a bit of a crunch. Add one-third of the egg white mixture to the melted chocolate and hand-whisk quickly and thoroughly. Using a rubber spatula or wooden spoon, fold in half of the remaining whites until most of the streaks are gone. Fold in the remaining whites and continue to mix until only a few streaks remain. Gently fold in the whipped cream.

Using a pastry bag with a large star tip, pipe the mousse into serving glasses and chill. Top with fresh berries, if desired.

EVEREST

440 South LaSalle Street, Loop
(312) 663-8920
WWW.EVERESTRESTAURANT.COM
OWNER: LETTUCE ENTERTAIN YOU
EXECUTIVE CHEF–PARTNER: JEAN JOHO

The culinary scene that Chicago enjoys today wouldn't be possible without the chefs of yesterday. Jean Joho was one of those chefs. But he has transcended his old-guard past to become part of the new guard as well, bridging the gap from classic to contemporary, not only in the evolution of his cooking style and of his restaurant that is the Chicago institution Everest, but also in his mentorship of culinary students and countless up-and-coming and now-successful chefs. Joho has also bridged the culinary generation gap with new endeavors like the remaking of his long-standing Brasserie Jo into Paris Club as a partner with Lettuce Entertain You Enterprises' Melman family.

The Melman family, which continues to own Everest where Joho serves as partner and executive chef, is perceived by many as one of the most influential restaurant families in the world. People agree Lettuce Entertain You also stands as one of the most successful restaurant enterprises not just in Chicago but in the country.

The Melman family and Lettuce Entertain You have spanned multiple generations, as Joho has. Founder Richard Melman's first restaurant in the seventies, a burger joint called R. J. Grunt's with its legendary salad bar. Melman later named his son after the eatery, R. J., who has followed in the family business as a restaurant owner and operator with his own

style, ideas, and agenda, all in a good way. Second son Jerrod and daughter Molly have also joined as partners and operators, working together to open the boisterous food-and-drink-focused Hub 51 and, later, Paris Club next door.

Since 1986 when Everest opened, Joho has led the natural progression from fine-dining French cuisine to a fresher approach with influences from Italy, Germany, and Switzerland—countries where Joho has lived and worked outside of his native France—still with the same sophistication and refinement that longtime regulars and newcomers expect. Another difference? Local farm foods are much easier to come by than years ago.

"When you compare the 1986 customers to the customers of today, today's customers are much more sophisticated," Joho says. "There are so many better restaurants in the city, people are used to a higher level of food and service. I just have to get better on a daily basis and try to improve something for the customer and for the staff, always."

The décor has evolved too, from old-school charm to a fresher, brighter, new-school feel "much more alive today than before," Joho says. And he's made sure that service isn't stuffy like the days of yore, but rather aimed at creating a comfortable, conversational experience.

"We're much better than we were ten years ago, we're much better than twenty-five years ago, and I know in five, ten years we'll be even better," Joho says. "We're not a trendy restaurant—we're really stable, and people who come here know what to expect, but they'll still get those little surprises that create a wonderful evening and keep them coming back."

A professionally trained pastry chef, Joho offers a dessert that draws upon his Alsatian background, evident in the rose hips, kirsch, and Gewürztraminer in the recipe, serving as a new-school interpretation of the classic apple beignet. Joho works with a farmer in Michigan to use heirloom Golden Star apples for this recipe, but any good-quality, crisp, semi-tart apple, such as Honey Crisp or Cortland, will do.

APPLE BEIGNETS WITH KIRSCH–FROMAGE BLANC ICE CREAM AND ROSE HIP GLAZE

(Serves 4)

For the ice cream:

2 cups light cream or half-and-half
1 vanilla bean, split lengthwise, or 2 teaspoons
   pure vanilla extract
5 large egg yolks
1/3 cup granulated sugar
8 ounces fromage blanc* or cream cheese
2 tablespoons granulated sugar
2 ounces kirsch**

For the beignets:

2 cups all-purpose flour
Pinch of salt
Pinch of sugar
2 large egg yolks
10 ounces beer
1 teaspoon canola oil
3 egg whites

For the rose hip glaze:

2 cups Alsatian Gewürztraminer wine
1 teaspoon rose hip liqueur***
4 Golden Star, Honey Crisp, or other crisp apples
Canola oil for frying
Cinnamon sugar for dusting

For the ice cream, in a saucepan over medium-high heat, bring the cream and vanilla to a simmer and turn off heat. In a medium bowl whisk the yolks and the sugar to a sandy consistency. Pour in a few tablespoons of the cream, whisking constantly. Gradually add the rest of the cream, still whisking constantly. Return mixture to saucepan over low heat, stirring with a wooden spoon until steam begins to form and mixture thickens to a heavy cream consistency, about 170–175°F. To prevent curdling the eggs, once it will coat the back of the spoon, immediately remove from the heat and strain through a fine mesh sieve, discarding the vanilla bean if used. Allow to cool. This crème anglaise or custard ice cream base can be covered with plastic wrap and refrigerated for up to two days.

Add the fromage blanc, sugar, and kirsch to the bowl with the crème anglaise, whisking to combine. Transfer mixture to an ice cream maker and prepare according to manufacturer's instructions. Freeze until serving.

For the beignet batter, in a large bowl, whisk together the flour, salt, sugar, and egg yolks. Pour in beer and oil and whisk until well combined. Refrigerate batter at least 15 minutes, up to overnight. Using a stand mixer, a handheld electric mixer, or a strong arm and a wire whisk, whip the egg whites until they form soft peaks. Fold into batter.

For the rose hip glaze, combine the wine and liqueur in a saucepan over medium-high heat and reduce until mixture has the consistency of syrup.

In a large saucepan, pour oil until it reaches 2 inches along the sides; heat to 375°F. Peel each apple and cut flesh with a small knife in a spiral. Sprinkle apple spirals with a touch of sugar and a dash of kirsch. Dredge each apple in the batter, shaking to remove excess, and fry until golden brown, about 1 minute. Drain on paper towels. Sprinkle beignets with cinnamon sugar.

To serve, spread the rose hip glaze evenly among four plates. Top with an apple beignet and serve with a scoop or quenelle of the kirsch ice cream.

Note: Fromage blanc, meaning "white cheese" in French, is a creamy, soft cheese with the consistency of thick yogurt or cream cheese, but with less fat. Cream cheese can be substituted in the recipe.

**Note:* Kirsch or kirschwasser is a clear German spirit made from distilled cherries. Not overly sweet, the spirit has a fruity aroma and a sharp bite and is often stirred into cheese fondues or taken as a shot when eating fondue to aid in digestion of the heavy dairy intake. Kirsch can be found in major liquor stores or specialty stores.

***Note:* Rose hip liqueur is made from rose hips, which are popular in Alsace, Sweden, and other colder climates, and are often used for medicinal purposes because of their high vitamin C component. The delicate liqueur has grown popular among cocktail artists and mixologists. Koval Distillery in Chicago produces a rose hip liqueur.

Mindy's Hot Chocolate

1747 North Damen Avenue, Bucktown
(773) 489-1747
www.hotchocolatechicago.com
Owner-Executive Chef: Mindy Segal

Pastry, chocolates, creams and sorbets, and the colorful combinations that can be made with these—this has been Mindy Segal's domain for more than fifteen years.

The dessert menu at Mindy's Hot Chocolate is playful, charming, nostalgic, and fun to get into, with names like One Banana Two Banana, Cakes-n-Shake, Thoughts on Peanut Butter Cup, and her most popular Chocolate Number #1 (64 percent), a warm chocolate soufflé tart with salted caramel ice cream and house-made pretzels. And then there's the lineup of hot chocolates to round out the night.

Segal's philosophy as a chef and restaurateur is sourcing the best possible ingredients, from chocolate to flour, but perhaps most important, she remains committed to local Illinois and Midwestern farms for her produce, meats, cheeses, and more, worked into a savory American menu. A top-rated burger uses Illinois Heartland Meats beef, while roast chicken comes from Gunthorp Farms in Indiana, with vegetables and garnishes changing frequently with the seasons to take advantage of the freshest foods at hand.

Young lovers and groups of friends, families and baby boomers huddle around candlelit tables and big goblets of breathing wine in this earthy and warm, low-lit space dressed in velvety chocolate browns like the sweets on the plates.

A graduate of Kendall College and mentor to so many others, Segal trained in the legendary kitchens of Charlie Trotter's and the former Spago and Gordon before helping Michael Kornick launch his iconic restaurant MK. It was there that Segal developed her following, loyal then, loyal now and always.

For her fans, she offers a healthier "doughnut," one made by retaining the pure shape of a peach, topped with seasonal berries and a sabayon, or custard. If a blowtorch happens to be on hand, caramelize the custard for a few seconds like a crème brûlée (some specialty retailers sell this tool for cooking). Alternatively, if desired, broil the custard for a few seconds, but make sure to use an oven-safe dish. Verjuice, an acidic grape juice used in French and Middle Eastern cuisines as a softer vinegar for deglazing and condiments, can be found in gourmet grocery stores, but if unavailable, use a good-quality white wine vinegar spiked with a drop or two of freshly squeezed lemon juice.

Grilled Marinated Doughnut Peaches with Lemon Sabayon and Poached Michigan Blueberries

(Serves 6)

For the peaches and blueberries:

6 doughnut peaches, pitted
½ cup peach liqueur or sweet dessert wine
1 tablespoon sugar
1 vanilla bean, split lengthwise
1 tablespoon verjuice
1 pinch cracked black pepper

For the lemon sabayon:

2 eggs
2 egg yolks
¼ cup granulated sugar
1 tablespoon water
¹/₃ cup freshly squeezed lemon juice
1 pint fresh blueberries

First, prepare the peaches. In a large bowl, combine liqueur, sugar, vanilla bean, verjuice, and pepper. Add peaches, tossing to coat. Let stand at room temperature, 1 hour. Before serving, prepare a grill at medium heat. Drain peaches, reserving liquid. Grill peaches, flipping occasionally until tender and slightly caramelized on both sides.

To prepare the sabayon, whisk together the eggs, yolks, sugar, water, and lemon juice in a large stainless steel bowl or in the upper pot of a double boiler. Over simmering water, whisk custard until thick and tripled in volume. When thickened, set bowl or pot over a bowl of ice and stir occasionally until cool. Set aside.

For the poached blueberries, pour reserved peach liquid into a shallow saucepan and bring to a boil. Turn heat down to a simmer, add blueberries, and continue to simmer very gently until tender.

To plate, divide warm, grilled peaches among shallow bowls or ramekins. In the center of each peach, place a tablespoon of blueberries with liquid. Top with sabayon. If available, use a blowtorch to caramelize the custard brûlée-style. Serve immediately.

Ria / Balsan

Ria
WALDORF ASTORIA CHICAGO
11 EAST WALTON STREET, GOLD COAST
(312) 880-4400
WWW.RIARESTAURANTCHICAGO.COM

Balsan
WALDORF ASTORIA CHICAGO
11 EAST WALTON STREET, GOLD COAST
(312) 646-1400
WWW.BALSANRESTAURANT.COM
EXECUTIVE CHEF: DANNY GRANT
EXECUTIVE PASTRY CHEF: STEPHANIE PRIDA

Ria shocked the city when it was awarded two highly prestigious stars by Michelin when the restaurant rating system made its debut in Chicago. This wasn't because the restaurant didn't deserve it; rather, the newbie had been open only seven months at the time and received the same award as the Peninsula Hotel's gem Avenues and the iconic Charlie Trotter's. Originally, Trotter planned to head up the sleek Elysian Hotel restaurant, but those plans fell through before it became Ria.

The award was quite an accomplishment, to be sure. Though chef Jason McCleod departed soon afterward, North Pond–trained chef de cuisine Danny Grant moved up to top rank and pastry chef Stephanie Prida stayed on to help maintain the kitchen's stellar reputation.

Backing up to Ria is Balsan, the casual Parisian-bistro-like eatery and oyster bar that shares the same kitchen and staff. That means Grant, Prida, and the rest of the team work hard, really hard. Not only do they support the hotel's room service and catering services, they must switch between two speeds for their dual restaurants—getting plates out briskly for Balsan, while pacing the courses more slowly at Ria.

To meet this volume and demand, the kitchen is set up like one of the ancient brigade systems founded by Auguste Escoffier, credited with updating and documenting the traditional French cooking techniques still taught in culinary schools around the world today. There is even a photo of Escoffier hanging prominently on one of the kitchen walls so no one forgets their place or mission in the kitchen.

For a somewhat "factory" operation, Grant, Prida, and team send out some of the most delicate, elegantly created and plated dishes in the city—and apparently, according to Michelin, in all of Western cuisine. The kitchen's stainless steel plating surface takes up what seems like fully half of the space, with everyone coming together to tweak, adjust, and perfect each dish before it goes out.

The minimalist cream-tinted dining room peppered by oversized paintings with just a splash of color provides a clean backdrop for the more elaborate artistry on the plates. Dan Pilkey, one of the youngest master sommeliers in the country, roams the dining room with a wide smile and encyclopedia of wine knowledge developed over fifteen years, which seems unlikely coming from this baby-faced charmer. Growing up in California and living and working in various wine countries helps.

When it comes to pastries, Prida combines the classic with the contemporary, as here in her traditional French, ultra-fluffy crepe cake enriched by a deep, custardy crème. She chooses to use whole wheat, less as a health factor than as a vehicle for adding a bit more texture and bite.

Whole Wheat Crepe Cake with Crescenza Custard

(serves 8–12)

For the custard:

3 sheets gelatin
8½ ounces egg yolks
7½ ounces sugar
1½ quarts heavy cream
12 ounces cream cheese, softened
11¾ ounces Crescenza cheese*, softened

For the batter and garnish:

8¼ cups milk, divided
4 ounces butter, plus more for cooking
6 ounces sugar
12 ounces all-purpose flour
12 ounces whole wheat flour
4 teaspoons salt
16 eggs
Powdered sugar (optional)
1½ cup fresh berries (optional)
5 basil leaves, sliced into a chiffonade (optional)

To prepare the custard, bloom the gelatin in cold water, about 5 minutes. Strain and set aside. Beat the egg yolks gently with the sugar in a medium bowl. In a saucepan over medium heat, heat the cream until gently simmering. Immediately reduce heat to medium-low. Ladle about ½ cup of the cream into the egg yolk mixture, whisking constantly to temper the eggs. Gently ladle in another ½ cup of the cream, whisking constantly, and then transfer the mixture back to the pot with the remaining cream over medium-low heat. Add the gelatin, continuing to whisk constantly until mixture is heated to 185°F and thick enough to coat the back of the spoon. Add the cream cheese and Crescenza cheese, stirring until melted. Cool in an ice bath and then refrigerate until completely chilled, about an hour or overnight.

Next, prepare the batter. Heat 2 cups of the milk and 4 ounces butter in a saucepan over medium-low heat until butter is melted. In a large bowl, combine the sugar, both flours, and salt, whisking to combine. Whisk in the eggs and remaining 6¼ cups milk. Gently pour in the warm milk mixture, whisking until combined. Chill completely in the refrigerator, about 1–2 hours, or overnight.

For the crepes, in a skillet over medium heat, melt 1 tablespoon butter and pour in a thin layer of the batter. Cook until set on one side, about 1–2 minutes. Flip, continuing to cook until the crepe is cooked through. Set aside. Repeat the process for 20 crepes, adding more butter to the pan as necessary to prevent sticking. Stack the completed crepes separated by wax paper. Chill crepes completely in the refrigerator.

To assemble the cake, spoon a thin layer of the cheese custard onto the first crepe. Top with another crepe and repeat the custard layering process until all 20 crepes have been used. Refrigerate for a half hour before slicing and serving. Before slicing and serving, dust with powdered sugar and top with fresh berries and basil, if desired.

*Note: Crescenza is a soft cow's milk cheese found in cheese shops, specialty grocery stores, or natural food markets. It has a buttery and rich flavor with tangy undertones.

BLACKBIRD

619 WEST RANDOLPH STREET, WEST LOOP
(312) 715-0708
WWW.BLACKBIRDRESTAURANT.COM
CO-OWNER–EXECUTIVE CHEF: PAUL KAHAN
CO-OWNER: DONNIE MADIA
CHEF DE CUISINE: DAVID POSEY
FORMER PASTRY CHEF: PATRICK FAHY

First, Charlie Trotter introduced modern American cuisine and the use of farm-focused foods to Chicago. Bruce Sherman expanded on that market-driven, seasonal cuisine with a serious focus on Illinois and other Midwestern farms. But it was Paul Kahan, along with innovative restaurateur Donnie Madia, who did both of those things, making market-driven, modern Midwest and American cuisine more approachable for the everyday diner.

To say it's "approachable" is not to say Blackbird is by any means a "casual" restaurant. Yet though it has a sleek, dressed-up interior and a stylish crowd, Blackbird certainly takes a lively and open attitude toward hospitality and service with a more upfront bar, full-spectrum wine list, youthful kitchen staff, and even a sense of playfulness with some of the menu's dishes.

A few years after the now more-than-a-decade-old Blackbird began raking in the awards and found its permanent footing, Paul Kahan relinquished control over the kitchen to chef de cuisine Michael Sheerin while he worked on expanding his restaurant empire and assuming a more business-focused role. Under Sheerin's leadership, which lasted until 2001 when the Chicago native and brother to Patrick Sheerin of Signature Room (page 147) left to start his own restaurant (see Movers and Shakers, page 183), Blackbird evolved into an even more modern and contemporary culinary institution.

Michael Sheerin's mark on the menu could be seen in the chemistry-like molecular gastronomy tricks he learned from Wylie Dufresne of WD~50 in New York blended on the same plate with more delicate, classic cooking. He might offer crispy sweetbreads placed prettily on narrow white china with bee pollen, fried chocolate, and spiced hazelnuts, or perhaps smoked duck liver with watermelon and barbecued green tomatoes, or shredded papaya "pasta" as the bed for a gently cooked sea bass.

When Sheerin left, the transition to former Blackbird sous-chef David Posey happened seamlessly. A Grant Achatz protégé, Posey also shows a scientific, yet elegant style. And in the pastry kitchen, which has been in several talented, award-winning hands, pastry chef Patrick Fahy in just his first year on the job earned many shout-outs in the press and was easily declared a rising star. Fahy, who trained with Thomas Keller at the French Laundry, one of the most renowned restaurants in the country, combines that mastery of fine-dining technique with the more hearty, wholesome, and playful pastry and baking style characteristic of his Midwestern roots. Though Fahy has since left his post at Blackbird, his creations live on as a harmonious blend of his many influences and experiences, shaped into a classic-meets-unique-meets-beautiful approach. His polenta pound cake is simple, seasonal, and distinctive at the same time, thanks to the slightly crunchy, savory polenta that provides more taste and textural interest than plain old flour and butter.

POLENTA POUND CUPCAKES WITH MASCARPONE "FROSTING" AND BERRIES

(Makes 12 cupcakes)

For the cupcakes:

1¼ cups unsalted butter
1¼ cups sugar
2 teaspoons salt
1 tablespoon vanilla extract
3 large eggs
1¼ cups all-purpose flour
½ cup cornmeal
1½ teaspoons baking powder
¾ cup sour cream

For the topping:

1 cup mascarpone
1 cup whipping cream
½ cup sugar
2 cups mixed berries or seasonal fruit
Powdered sugar (optional)

Preheat the oven to 350°F.

Grease a standard-size muffin pan with butter or cooking spray and dust lightly with flour or use paper liners.

In an electric stand mixer fitted with the paddle attachment, beat together the butter, sugar, and salt on medium-high speed until light, fluffy, and pale in color. Add the vanilla, followed by the eggs.

In a separate bowl, whisk together the flour, cornmeal, and baking powder. Fold in half of these dry ingredients into the wet mixture until well combined. Fold in the sour cream, followed by the remaining half of the dry ingredients until no more visible flour remains.

Fill the cupcake molds with the batter until about three-quarters full.

Bake cupcakes for 30 minutes or until knife or toothpick comes out clean. Baking times will vary by oven, so check the cupcakes after the first 15 minutes.

Cool cupcakes thoroughly on a wire rack, about 30–45 minutes. Meanwhile, whisk together the mascarpone, whipping cream, and sugar in a bowl or electric stand mixer until stiff peaks form.

Spread mascarpone "frosting" evenly on the tops of the cooled cupcakes. Top with berries and dust with powdered sugar, if desired. Alternatively, you can bake this in layer cake form.

AVEC

Avec, directly next door to Blackbird, opened in 2003 with a bold new approach to eating and drinking. Wrapped in pure, light wood, with wooden walls and banquettes and a long wooden bar, Avec was Kahan and Madia's "casual" solution to the rarity of restaurants where the everyday diner could access the quality cooking of a fine-dining-trained chef.

It was also the first restaurant to introduce communal dining and shared eating. The term "small plates," long before it became mainstream, was introduced by Avec, where a paper menu changing daily and weekly looked like an extra-long appetizer list, or a deconstructed tasting menu of sorts, and where entrees were meant to be served family style, even if between two people. Kahan and Madia found that the naturally narrow space lent itself to long banquettes with close-together seats on one side and a long bar on the other where diners could easily meet new people. What came of that was, and is, a boisterous and breezy restaurant, thanks to inside-outside, all-glass storefront doors that open onto a waiting area on the patio.

In the exposed short-order-like kitchen, Koren Grieveson has focused on sourcing local produce and foods, cooking and presenting these ingredients simply in a rather Mediterranean style that enhances, not changes, the original, authentic flavors. For her brandade, salt cod is whipped to airiness and served simply alongside homemade garlic bread and fresh herbs. A seared red snapper comes with bulgur wheat salad, caramelized brussels sprouts, a splash of sesame oil, and a vinaigrette spiked with salty bottarga caviar. When Avec opened, Grieveson also came to be known as the charcuterie and cheese expert—making her own cured meats and sourcing the best Midwestern, Californian, and imported cheeses she could, again serving those family style on cheerful chopping boards for the sharing.

In August of 2010 a building fire and subsequent tragic accident that killed a firefighter closed the restaurant, challenging its reopening as well as the spirit and hearts of its team. But the Kahan family recharged and reopened with Grieveson again at the helm, stronger, better, and certainly busier than before. If the side-by-side restaurants on Randolph Street weren't already a portrait of modern Chicago cuisine, they certainly are now.

SABLE KITCHEN & BAR

HOTEL PALOMAR
505 NORTH STATE STREET, RIVER NORTH
(312) 755-9704
WWW.SABLECHICAGO.COM
OWNER: KIMPTON HOTELS
EXECUTIVE CHEF: HEATHER TERHUNE

Heather Terhune makes her own sugar-spiced beef jerky. She uses sweet corn for an appetizer crème brûlée; combines grapefruit with avocado, crispy rock shrimp, romaine, and basil; pairs pickled apricots with classic pork rillettes; fries calamari with a graham cracker breading; blends bacon with sugar for a jam spread on toasted baguette with triple cream cheese.

Clearly a pastry chef at heart, Terhune effortlessly blends the sweet with the savory in her semi-Midwestern, semi-Southern, semi–New American comfort food menu. From beginning to end it is reflective of her work, residency, and travels throughout the country. And that ending comes with more comfort and nostalgia, in dark chocolate whoopee pies with a vanilla bean shake, local Burton Farms maple syrup tart with bourbon ice cream, easy rhubarb crumble, butterscotch pot de crème, and other fun flavors and treats.

In terms of menu design, Sable skips the overused "small plates" term, calling the dishes "social plates" instead. A descendent of tapas, the menu is divided into cleverly named sections meant for tasting and sharing, from Hors d'Oeuvres with the "snacky" mini-plates Terhune has fun with, to Fish, to Farm & Garden for veggies and salads, to Meat, to Flatbreads.

Sable is an eating and drinking establishment where those two things are meant precisely to go hand in hand. The mixology-focused cocktail program breaks down into categories of classic and newly created drinks that are warmed, spicy, sweet, and gentle for easy pairing throughout the course of a meal. And a huge, exposed kitchen line, with Terhune at the center, offers an exciting show throughout it all.

MINI CARROT CAKES WITH RUM-SOAKED RAISINS
(Makes 6 mini bundt cakes)

1½ cups raisins
½ cup dark rum
6 eggs
3 cups granulated sugar
1½ cups vegetable oil
2 pounds carrots, peeled and grated
4 cups all-purpose flour
1 tablespoon baking soda
1 teaspoon salt
1 tablespoon cinnamon
1 cup chopped walnuts, toasted
1 tablespoon pure vanilla extract
1 tablespoon powdered sugar (optional)

Soak raisins in rum for at least a few hours, or overnight.

Preheat oven to 350°F. In a large bowl, beat eggs lightly with a wooden spoon. Stir in sugar, oil, and grated carrots. Sift in flour, baking soda, salt, and cinnamon, folding until well combined. Fold in walnuts, vanilla, and rum-soaked raisins.

Grease 6 nonstick mini bundt cake pans with butter or cooking spray. Spoon batter into pans. Bake 20–25 minutes, or until the cake springs back and a toothpick inserted in the middle comes out with sticky crumbs. Cool completely on a wire rack. Unmold onto plates. If desired, dust cakes lightly with powdered sugar shaken through a strainer.

New York. Los Angeles. And now, Chicago. Each week it seems as if a new restaurant opens while another one closes, a chef leaves a post here and begins another there. But in Chicago, these chefs don't just move around. They make their lasting imprints at each place they touch, noticeable in the menus, the ambience and the feel of a restaurant that blends seamlessly into that of the next chef on board. And, unlike other cities, Chicago chefs may move around a bit, but nonetheless, they stay in the city. All of these little tremors of activity are precisely what make the culinary scene here so fresh and exciting, so transformative and current, and so blossoming at the same time.

DALE LEVITSKI

Dale Levitski knows all about moving and shaking. After training at the revered Trio, which in its two decades of existence saw the likes of Rick Tramonto and Gale Gand, Shawn McClain and Grant Achatz, Levitski moved over to the now-shuttered La Tache, where he refined his technique and began developing what would be his funky-creative, playful style. He later bounced around to consult on the menu for Orange, a now-icon brunch spot, as well as at Stone Lotus, a nightclub with a chef-driven menu. But Levitski's biggest move yet would be to leave Chicago altogether to be a contestant on the popular Bravo! TV *Top Chef* show, which was just getting its legs that third season. Levitski fared well but was ultimately voted off.

Then there was a quiet period while Levitski took time to deal with the passing of his mother and to figure out his next moves. When an idea for a contemporary American restaurant didn't pan out in the nationwide recession of 2008 that closed many city restaurants and tied up funding, Levitski pressed on and was later recruited for the executive chef position at local/organic-food-focused Sprout in Lincoln Park.

It was the move that made it for Levitski, who did more than just head up the kitchen. He turned a soon-to-close restaurant that would have gone down as a short-lived, overpriced, and, some say, poorly executed concept into a flourishing, approachable yet refined, fine-dining yet casual, sophisticated yet fresh little space—just the place for the whimsical approach, bubbly personality, and overtly sarcastic humor that have since made him a national TV chef celebrity.

"Careerwise, the biggest challenge I've had is overcoming my own personal insecurities and believing in the worthiness of what I'm doing," Levitski says. "I'm very proud of the work we're doing, but to get to this place, it's a hard road—you have to work hard and break through barriers to become a great chef." Just as *Top Chef* was about "doing the impossible" in Levitski's eyes, beating the high odds of failing in this competitive industry is doing just the same.

ROBERT AND ALLISON LEVITT

Rob and Allie Levitt are two more names easily associated with the "mover and shaker" idea, abruptly leaving their restaurant Mado a scant three years after opening and earning high accolades from major food magazines that same year. It was a bold move—the husband-wife chef team left the rough, daily restaurant grind altogether to open up a much-anticipated boutique butcher shop, Butcher & Larder, in the up-and-coming Noble Square neighborhood just east of Wicker Park and west of the expressway.

"We're doing it the old-school way," Rob says, referring to the handful of traditional butcher shops still in existence around the city and the niche the Levitts have carved for themselves—sustainably raised, whole-animal butchery with plenty of standard cuts, offcuts, and specialty items, plus a daily hot lunch with a limited menu that has included porchetta sandwiches with arugula and pickled onions, grown-up Sloppy Joes, chili, pozole, and more.

"This is something Chicago needed more of, and people have been really receptive to it. We noticed we were doing more butchery at the restaurant and less cooking, so we knew this would be a natural next move."

Inside the small storefront extending back to the coolers, Rob mans the in-plain-view butcher block, heaving giant hogs onto the boards for slicing and dicing into various products, including the more unusual cuts that restaurants and chefs love and that home cooks can't normally get, from fat-capped pork chops and thick-cut pork belly to a slew of homemade sausages, including chorizo. Brave home cooks can even take pig-butchering classes offered by the Levitts. But aside from pork, the duo's known for a wide range of other meats and specialty creations, like beef heart and house-made, house-cured charcuterie.

MICHAEL SHEERIN

Michael Sheerin, a Chicago native who had trained under molecular gastronomy master Wylie Dufresne in New York City, left his high-profile post as chef de cuisine at Paul Kahan's renowned Blackbird to work on opening his own restaurant, a long-held dream.

Sheerin started by getting some traction as a solo act, consulting on menu pairings for Indiana-based Three Floyds Brewery and developing ideas for what would be his new restaurant, the Trencherman. There resulted an evolution from "gastropub" items for Three Floyds like Parmesan-crusted pork rinds and spiced beef jerky into more refined creations that showcase Sheerin's penchant for scientific cookery and artistic presentation using core Midwestern farmers'-market finds. Sheerin continued to build steam for his new place by opening "pop-up" renditions of the Trencherman, showing off menu items as a guest chef here and there.

The pop-up idea, a growing phenomenon in Chicago, first took shape right after the recession hit, when new restaurants struggled to gather funds. Now it has become a way for chefs to build a core of preopening followers to ensure instant success when the doors open.

This was not unlike the strategy Stephanie Izard employed to build anticipation for Girl & the Goat when it was in the works, hosting underground dinners to which tickets sold in seconds, all the while blogging and tweeting about the restaurant's progress. Sheerin, Izard, and countless other chefs have demonstrated their cooking prowess in other "pop-up" ways too, mainly in the shape of numerous special events that have taken hold of the city each year, from fundraising dinners and tastings to themed events like Baconfest, the annual celebration of smoked and cured swine.

RICK TRAMONTO

In perhaps the biggest move of all, Rick Tramonto, the founder of nationally acclaimed Tru with ex-wife and business partner Gale Gand, shipped out to New Orleans, where he collaborated with Creole authority John Folse to open Restaurant R'evolution at the Royal Sonesta Hotel in the heart of the French Quarter, the first of several joint projects planned.

The two bonded in the wake of Hurricane Katrina, when Tramonto traveled south to help feed survivors and rescuers. They call their menu cross-cultural fusion, made up of modern, imaginative reinterpretations of classic Cajun and Creole cuisine. And just as Tramonto looked to capitalize on local Midwestern foods when in Chicago, he does the same in the Big Easy, with a focus on Gulf-caught Louisiana seafood, including playful dishes like "A Tale of Three Fishes," a study of French bouillabaisse and other seafood stews, alongside new takes on shrimp and grits, gumbo, jambalaya, and beignets. There are rumors that Rick's move to New Orleans may not be permanent . . .

Café des Architectes

Sofitel Chicago Water Tower
20 East Chestnut Street, Gold Coast
(312) 324-4000
www.cafedesarchitectes.com
Executive Chef: Greg Biggers
Executive Pastry Chef: Patrick Fahy (formerly Meg Galus)

Tucked quietly in the futuristic-looking trapezoid of white and clear glass that is the Sofitel hotel in Chicago's trendy, affluent Gold Coast neighborhood, Café des Architectes has focused on a fine-dining, French-inspired menu first shaped by Martial Noguier (Bistronomic, page 14). That menu has been even more modernized by incoming chef Greg Biggers.

And in the pastry kitchen former pastry chef Meg Galus, who worked under Gale Gand of Tru (page 164) once showed the breadth of her experience as a longtime baker and pastry chef classically trained at Chicago's French Pastry School, combining the influences from her Midwestern roots with elegant plating techniques.

A chocolate master, Galus specializes in classic French technique for handcrafting truffles and bonbons. Even as a child growing up in rural Illinois she did the same, creating whimsical desserts out of animal crackers and cake mixes at her imaginary "restaurant" for her parents and family.

Here Galus offers a simple, classic French cake originating in the Basque region. A layered cake typically filled with a fruit compote, the cake almost resembles a more rustic cherry pie—two thin rounds of buttery, shortbread-like dough encasing a thick, chunky filling.

Gateau Basque
(Makes 1 8-inch cake)

For the pastry dough:

7 tablespoons unsalted butter, at room
   temperature
3 tablespoons sugar
¼ teaspoon salt
²/₃ cup almond flour
2 teaspoons baking powder
1 egg
½ teaspoon vanilla extract
1 cup all-purpose flour

For the lemon cream:

½ cup milk
½ cup heavy cream
2 teaspoons finely grated lemon zest
4 egg yolks
¼ cup sugar
2 teaspoons all-purpose flour
2 teaspoons cornstarch
1½ tablespoons unsalted butter,
   room temperature

For the cherry compote:

4 cups pitted sweet cherries
¼ cup sugar
2 tablespoons water

To make the dough, in small bowl of electric mixer fitted with the paddle attachment, whip the butter, sugar, and salt on high speed until light and fluffy. Add the almond flour and baking powder; mix on low speed until combined. Add the egg and vanilla; continue to mix on low speed. Slowly add the all-purpose flour. When no more flour streaks remain and dough is slightly sticky in texture, remove the bowl and chill for at least 4 hours.

Meanwhile, prepare the lemon cream. In a small saucepan, bring the milk, cream, and lemon zest just to a boil; remove from heat and cool slightly. In a medium bowl, whisk together egg yolks, sugar, flour, and cornstarch until well blended. Gradually whisk the warm milk mixture into the egg mixture. Transfer back into the same saucepan. Cook over medium-high heat, whisking constantly until boiling. Continue to whisk for 1 more minute of boiling, until shiny and thick. Remove from heat; whisk in butter. Refrigerate until cooled completely.

To prepare the cherry compote, combine cherries, sugar, and water in a medium saucepan. Cook over medium heat, stirring occasionally, until cherries burst and release their liquid. Continue to cook until water is absorbed and mixture is thickened to jam consistency. Cool completely at room temperature.

To assemble the cake, roll out two-thirds of the dough to a 10-inch circle between two sheets of parchment paper. Roll remaining dough to an 8-inch circle. (If dough gets soft, return it to the refrigerator or freezer for a few minutes.) Press larger circle of dough into an 8-inch tart or cake pan, covering the bottom and about 1½ inches up sides of pan. Spread cherry compote evenly on dough; top with lemon cream. Place smaller circle of dough over filling, sealing the edges and pricking the top with a fork several times. Refrigerate 1 hour. Heat oven to 325°F. Bake until deep golden brown, about 30 minutes. Serve slightly warm with vanilla ice cream or cherry sorbet and fresh fruit. The photo shows the restaurant's individual serving.

INDEX

About the Author

Born and raised in Chicago, Amelia Levin has been a freelance writer covering her native city's culinary and nightlife scene for almost ten years. She regularly contributes to the *Chicago Sun-Times* and *Edible Chicago* magazine as well as to various food and restaurant industry trade publications. She has also written articles for the *Chicago Tribune, Metromix* (*Chicago Tribune*'s dining and entertainment site), *Chicago Life* magazine and *Citysearch,* among other outlets. Amelia has also written the dining section for the *Chicago Official Visitors Guide,* released by the Chicago Convention and Tourism Board.

As a certified chef through Kendall College in Chicago, Amelia develops and tests recipes for a number of clients and media outlets, including Oxmoor House's *Cooking Light: Fresh Food Fast* cookbook series.

As a result of her work, Amelia has developed hundreds of personal and professional relationships with Chicago-area chefs, restaurateurs, bar owners, caterers, food and beverage directors, and other culinarians in the city.

Amelia is an active member of the International Association of Culinary Professionals (IACP) and serves on the board of directors for the International Food Editorial Council (IFEC). She was also an award winner at the 2009 Greenbriar Symposium for Professional Food Writers and has served as a judge for a number of culinary and food-writing competitions. During the warmer months, she helps out at the Green City Market, Chicago's largest farmers' market.

Read more about Amelia at www.amelialevin.com.